GET THEE TO A PUNNERY

William Shakespeare, punster without peer,
knew it. And Richard Lederer proves it in an
irrepressible exploration of puns that
becomes a wit-sharpening adventure from
cover to cover.

From poetic licenses of *bon motorists* (vanity
plates) to knock-knock jokes; from the word
finagling of famous punsters to spoonerisms;
from genus puns to genius punnery of all
kinds in advertising, literature, and life,
Lederer reveals and revels in the art of the
pun—to the delectation of all.

GET THEE TO A PUNNERY

The Intrepid Linguist

ANGUISHED ENGLISH
IT'S RAINING CATS AND DOGS
GET THEE TO A PUNNERY

Get Thee To a Punnery

by
Richard Lederer

Illustrations
by
Bill Thompson

A LAUREL BOOK
Published by
Dell Publishing
a division of
Bantam Doubleday Dell Publishing Group, Inc.
666 Fifth Avenue
New York, New York 10103

ISBN: 0-440-20499-2

Reprinted by arrangement with Wyrick & Company

Printed in the United States of America

Published simultaneously in Canada

January 1990

10 9 8 7 6 5 4 3 2 1

OPM

Contents

This way, my lord, for this way lies the game.

William Shakespeare,
King Henry the Sixth

Game Notes

I n the arrangement of the twenty-five games in this book there is method to the madness, as well as madness in the method. After the first chapters on the pervasive punnery in our lives come several games involving punnish signs and license plates that we see all around us. Next appears "A Primer of Puns," followed by games that play with the three major types of pun-making—homographs, homophones, and double sound puns. This basic taxonomy is solidified by an extensive test of the reader's punupmanship.

There follows another cluster of games progressing from single sound puns, such as "Have You Ever Seen a Horse Fly?", to double sound puns, such as "Anguish Languish." Then the book closes with two more types of punnery—meld puns and spoonerisms—and a generous round of set-up puns that reviews all the methods presented in the first nineteen chapters.

Any good game consists of items of varying levels of difficulty. Some of the punning posers are likely to stump you the first time around, but you will find that insights into the more challenging questions will come to you in sudden flashes when you return to the games a second and third time.

When you are sure that you have reached your limit, turn to the back of the book, where answers to all the games repose.

Versions of some of the games in this book have appeared in *Diversion*, *Writing!*, and *Word Ways* and have been revised and expanded with permission.

A good pun may be admitted among the small excellencies of lively conversation.

James Boswell

In Praise of Puns

Believe it or not, early in January of each year America celebrates National Save the Pun Week. About this occasion Dan Carlinsky has observed, "Most folks will probably think that celebrating the pun is about as worthwhile as celebrating a hangnail or a full garbage pail. The pun is the most misunderstood and most beset-upon form of humor."

I have written this book to sweep away all misunderstandings about the crafty art of punnery and to convince you that the pun is well worth celebrating—all year round. After all, the pun is mightier than the sword, and these days you are much more likely to run into a pun than into a sword.

Scoffing at puns seems to be a conditioned reflex, and through the centuries a steady barrage of libel and slander has been aimed at the practice of punning. Nearly three hundred years ago John Dennis sneered, "A pun is the lowest form of wit," a charge that has been butted and rebutted by a mighty line of pundits and punheads.

Henry Erskine, for example, has protested that if a pun is the lowest form of wit, "it is, therefore, the foundation of all wit." Oscar Levant has added a tagline: "A pun is the lowest form of humor – when you don't think of it first." John Crosbie and Bob Davies have responded to Dennis with hot, cross puns: "The pun has been said to be the lowest form of humus – earthy wit that everyone digs" and "If someone complains that punning is the lowest form of humor, you can tell them that poetry is verse."

Samuel Johnson, the eighteenth century self-appointed custodian of the English language, once thundered, "To trifle with the vocabulary which is the vehicle of social intercourse is to tamper with the currency of human intelligence. He who would violate the sanctities of his Mother Tongue would invade the recesses of the national till without remorse."

If language is money and language manipulators are thieves, Doctor Johnson was a felon, for to him is attributed the following:

> I should be punishéd
> For every pun I shed:
> Do not leave a puny shred
> Of my punnish head!

thus proving the truth of Joseph Addison's pronouncement: "The seeds of Punning are in the minds of all men, and tho' they may be subdued by Reason, Reflection, and good Sense, they will be very apt to shoot up in the greatest Genius, that is not broken and cultivated by the rules of Art."

Far from being invertebrate, the inveterate punster is a brave entertainer. He or she loves to create a three-ring circus of words: words clowning, words teetering on tightropes, words swinging from tent-tops, words thrusting their heads into the mouths of lions. Punnery can be highly entertaining, but it is always a risky business. The humor can fall on its face, it can lose its balance and plunge into the sawdust, or it can be decapitated by the snapping shut of jaws.

While circus performers often receive laughter or applause for their efforts, punsters often draw an obligatory groan for theirs. But the fact that most people groan at rather than laugh at puns doesn't mean that the punnery isn't funnery. If the pun is a good one, the groan usually signifies a kind of suppressed admiration for the verbal acrobatics on display, and perhaps a hidden envy.

Edgar Allan Poe (of all people) neatly (and ravenously?) summed up the situation when he wrote, with all his tell-tale heart, "Of puns it has been said that those most dislike who are least able to utter them." Almost a century later, Henry Fowler, in his *Dictionary of Modern English Usage*, expanded on Poe's insight: "The assumption that puns are *per se* contemptible, betrayed by the habit of describing every pun not as 'a pun,' but as 'a bad pun' or 'a feeble pun,' is a sign at once of sheepish docility and a desire to seem superior. Puns are good, bad, and indifferent, and only those who lack the wit to make them are unaware of the fact."

So hurry! hurry! hurry! Step right up and into a circus of words. All the humor will be in tents, guaranteed to whet (and wet) your appetite for more. Chew a little at a time. After you've digested this book, you'll find that, indeed, a bun is the doughiest form of wheat.

In the beginning was the pun.
Samuel Beckett

The Word Play's the Thing

The best place to start is to face up to the fact that you have been uttering, hearing, and reading puns most of your life.

When you were very young, you probably chanted songs like:

> Fuzzy Wuzzy was a bear.
> Fuzzy Wuzzy had no hair.
> Fuzzy Wuzzy wasn't fuzzy, was he?

and:

> A sailor went to C-C-C,
> To see what he could C-C-C,
> But all that he could C-C-C
> Was the bottom of a great blue C-C-C.

From a grown-up's point of view such ditties may seem to be rather primitive examples of language play. But these songs, which have become so much a part of our oral folk culture, actually represent the child's first attempts to put into memorable form his or her pleasure in discovering that the same sound can suggest two diverse meanings—*wuzzy* and *was he*; *C*, *sea*, and *see*.

As you were growing up, it was on riddles that you really began to cut your punning eye teeth (which Clifton Fadiman calls *bon mot*-lars). In *Word*

Play, Peter Farb explains that "the majority of American children are strikingly punctual in acquiring a repertoire of riddles at about age six or seven."

Unless you were raised as a hermit (or, if you are male, a hismit), you probably recognize many of these traditional riddles:

- What's black and white and red (read) all over?
  A newspaper.
- What did the letter say to the stamp?
  Stick with me and we'll go places.
- What kind of shoes are made from banana skins?
  Slippers.
- How do you know when it's raining cats and dogs?
  When you step in a poodle.
- When is a door not a door?
  When it's ajar.
- What kind of rooms have no walls?
  Mushrooms.
- What happened to the boy who drank 8 Cokes?
  He burped 7-Up.
- At what time of day was Adam created?
  A little before Eve.
- Who was the most popular actor in the Bible?
  Samson. He brought down the house.
- Where do ghosts receive their mail?
  At the dead letter office.

Early in your career as a punster you discovered certain categories of riddles, like the Silly Billy (or moron) posers and the irrepressible elephant jokes. How many of these classic two-liners do you recognize?:

- Why did Silly Billy throw the clock out the window?
  He wanted to see time fly.

- Why did Silly Billy throw the butter out the window?
  He wanted to see the butter fly.

- Why did Silly Billy take a ladder to the ballpark?
  He wanted to see the Giants play.

- Why didn't Silly Billy open the refrigerator?
  He was embarrassed to see the salad dressing.

- Why did Silly Billy jump off the Empire State Building?
  He wanted to make a smash hit on Broadway.

- How do you make an elephant float?
  Use a scoop of ice cream, some root beer, and an elephant.

- Where do elephants store their clothes?
  In their trunks.

- What happens to a grape when an elephant steps on it?
  It lets out a little whine.

- How can you stop an elephant from charging?
  Take away its credit card.

- Who are the two greatest elephant singers?
  Harry Elephante and Elephant Gerald.

Soon you graduated to other forms of juvenile humor—the Confucius-say jokes, the author-and-book jokes, and, of course, the everpresent knock-knock jokes: Knock, Knock. Who's there? Pencil. Pencil who? Pencil fall down if you don't wear suspenders.

As you were sharpening your punupmanship by

chanting songs, posing riddles, and dropping one-liners, all around you the mass media were creating catchy and catching messages, especially in advertisements. The language of advertising is language on the make, and an astonishing number of ads use puns to make a point and to make a buck:

- Gets the red out. – Visine
- Take Aim against cavities. – Aim toothpaste
- Thousands of surefire lights. – Cricket lighters
- The cure for the common cola. – 7-Up
- Milk does a body good. – American Dairy Association

Public service messages employ puns to make serious points, as these highway safety signs illustrate:

- Children should be seen and not hurt.
- Be wreckless, not reckless.
- Be patient today, not a patient tomorrow.
- If you love your kid, belt him.
- He who has one for the road gets trooper for chaser.

In the classroom, punnery abounds in the greatest of literary works. In the ninth book of Homer's *Odyssey*, composed about 800 B.C., the wily Odysseus is trapped in the cave of Polyphemus, the one-eyed giant with 20/ vision. To fool the Cyclops, Odysseus gives his name as Outis, Greek for "No Man."

When Odysseus attacks the giant in order to escape from the cave, Polyphemus calls to his fellow monsters for help, crying, "No man is killing me!" Naturally, his colleagues take him literally and make no attempt to aid him. In this way, Polyphemus falls victim to one of the first puns in European literature.

The Catholic Church is founded on another Greek pun, this one in *Matthew* 16:18, where Jesus says, "Thou art Peter (*petros*), and upon this rock (*petra*) I will build my church."

Victor Margolin observes that "in the art of punning, Shakespeare was great shakes and without peer," and estimates of the number of puns in the Bard's published works range from 1,000 to 3,000.

In the opening scene of *Julius Caesar*, a commoner identifies himself as a cobbler, "a mender of bad soles," and adds, "Truly sir, all I live by is with the awl: I meddle with no tradesman's matters, nor women's matters, but with awl. I am indeed, sir, a surgeon to old shoes; when they are in great danger, I recover them."

In *Hamlet*, the Prince of Denmark's first three speeches turn on puns as emblems of his rapier riposting wit. While the court around him makes merry, Hamlet continues to wear black to mourn the untimely death of his father and the hasty marriage of his mother, the Queen, to his uncle, King Claudius:

King:
But now my cousin Hamlet, and my son—

Hamlet:
A little more than kin and less than kind.

King:
How is it that the clouds still hang on you?

Hamlet:
Not so, my lord, I am too much in the 'son'.

Queen:

Good Hamlet, cast thy nighted color off,
And let thine eye look like a friend on
Denmark.
Do not forever with thy veiléd lids
Seek for thy noble father in the dust.
Thou know'st 'tis common, all that lives must
die,
Passing through nature to eternity.

Hamlet:

Ay, madam, it is common.

Shakespeare was never beneath tossing a pun into the most serious of scenes. After Macbeth has murdered King Duncan, Lady Macbeth says, with forked meaning, "If he do bleed, I'll gild the faces of the grooms withal. For it must seem their guilt." And in *Romeo and Juliet* the stabbed Mercutio expires with a pun on his bleeding lips: "Ask for me to-morrow and you shall find me a grave man."

Referring to ages such as the English Renaissance, sociologist G. C. Lichtenberg has observed that "where the common people like puns, and make them, the nation is on a high level of culture." If this is true, American culture in the late twentieth century is indeed in full bloom. All around us puns spring up like flowers (the scoffers would say like weeds), and our lives become a little more fragrant when we examine how these puns germinate and grow.

That is just what this book is designed to do.

> *Nothing is more foolish than to talk of frivolous things seriously; but nothing is wittier than to make frivolities serve serious ends.*
>
> Erasmus

The Time of the Signs

Language is fun. Everyone who speaks and listens and writes and reads is involved to some degree with the inherent playfulness of human language. Ancient graffiti, classical fables, and many stories from the Bible and mythology show us that people have played with language for a very long time. But never before have so many of us enjoyed the game of words and tried to play it ourselves.

A vivid example occurred during the last day of the 1987 Wimbledon tennis championships. The finals pitted the eleventh-seeded Australian Pat Cash against the top player in the world, Czechoslovakian Ivan Lendl. Surprisingly, the Aussie won in straight sets, and as he was closing out his victory, two spectators held up a sign that read, "Cash is better than a Czech."

Here are various placards and posters that have appeared around the world. Both literally and figuratively they are signs of our times, times in which we human beings love to fiddle with words and to laugh at the loony tunes that such fiddling produces:

- *On a diaper service truck*: Rock a dry baby.
- *On an electric company van*: Power to the people.
- *On a plumber's truck*: A flush is better than a full house.
- *In a beauty parlor*: Curl up and dye.
- *In front of a church*: Stop here for your holiday spirits.
- *On a church lawn*: Pray keep off the grass. Such trespasses will *not* be forgiven.
- *In a Catholic church*: Litany candles?
- *In a bar*: I'm not a slow bartender. I'm not a fast bartender. I'm a half fast bartender.
- *In another bar*: Marriage consoler.
- *In an ice cream and dairy store*: You can't beat our milk shakes, but you can whip our cream and lick our ice cream cones.
- *On a fortune-teller's door*: Medium prices.
- *On a junkyard fence*: Edifice wrecks.
- *On a motel*: Dew Drop Inn.
- *In the window of a necktie emporium*: Come in and tie one on.
- *In a sporting goods store*: How about a boomerang for the girl who returns everything?
- *Over a display of batteries*: Wanna start something?
- *Outside a strip tease theater*: Here the belles peel.
- *On a peanut stand*: If our peanuts were any fresher, they'd be insulting.
- *Over an antique shop*: Remains to be seen.

- *With a display of leftover Christmas decorations*: All that glitters was not sold.

- *At a tire store*: Time to re-tire.

- *In a bookstore window*: Curdle up with a good mystery.

- *In a supermarket*: Prices are born here and raised elsewhere.

- *On a southern street*: No U-all turns.

- *Outside a chromium factory*: There's no plate like chrome.

- *In a music store window*: Guitars for sale. Cheap. No strings attached.

- *On the door of another music store*: Gone Chopin. Bach in a minuet.

- *On an ecology T-shirt*: Urban sprawl is the forest's prime evil.

- *At a poultry farm*: Better laid than ever.

- *Outside an amusement park*: Children under 14 must be accompanied by money and daddy.

- *In a brassiere shop*: We fix flats.

- *In a window display of brassieres*: We're the real decoy.

- *In a real estate office*: Get lots for little.

- *In two travel agencies*: Let yourself go. Please go away!

- *On a market stall*: Lovely glass paperweights. The only way to keep your household bills down.

- *Over a bargain basement counter*: What you seize is what you get.

- *In a savings bank*: No deposit — no return.

- *In a butcher shop window*: No two weighs about it.
- *In another such window*: Never a bum steer.
- *In a dentist's office*: Get your new plates here.
- *In a sportswear shop*: Buy a girl a bikini. It's the least you can do for her.
- *In a shoe store*: Come in and have a fit.
- *On a divorce lawyer's wall*: Satisfaction guaranteed or your honey back.
- *In a lumberyard*: Come see, come saw.
- *In a pet store window*: Merry Christmas and a Yappy New Year.
- *In a car rental agency*: Love 'em and lease 'em.
- *At a swimming pool*: Welcome to our ool. You notice there's no P in it. Please keep it that way.
- *On a garbage truck*: Your garbage is our bread and butter.
- *In a garden shop*: We're a growing concern.

Among the most verbally vivacious are those signs found on and in restaurants:

- Protect your bagels. Put lox on them.
- Close door. Wonderful draught inside.
- Frank 'n Stein.
- Ice cold beer. Great relief pitcher.
- Garden of Eating.
- Pizza on Earth.
- Don't stand outside and be miserable. Come inside and be fed up.
- Buy now. Pay waiter.

You have to give the creators of these signs credit for their bright humor and beguiling word play. But if you ask for credit, you may meet a sign that says, "Credit cheerfully refused" or "Try our easy payment plan. 100 percent down. No future worries about payment" or "Credit extended to anyone over 80 who is accompanied by a parent."

Now let's see how much credit you can gain in the quiz that follows. Here are twenty more authentic signs that punder for business. In each blank write the missing word. Then check your answers with the puns that appear in the back of this book.

1. *In a junkyard*: Rust in _____.

2. *By a motel*: Come in and take a _____ off your mind.

3. *On an antique shop*: Den of _____.

4. *At a tire store*: We _____you not.

5. *At a planetarium*: Cast of thousands. Every one a _____.

6. *On a church bulletin board*: This church is _____ conditioned.

7. *In front of another church*: Come in and get your _____ lifted.

8. *In a tailor shop*: We'll clean you. We'll press you. We'll even _____ for you.

9. *Outside an optician's shop*:_____ for sore eyes.

10. *On a newly seeded lawn*: Don't ruin the gay young _____.

11. *In a jewelry store*: There's no present like the _____.

12. *In the window of a watch repair shop*: If it doesn't tick, _____ to us.

13. *In a billiard parlor window*: Try our indoor_____.

14. *In a furrier's window*: Be our miss in _____.

15. *On the wall of a dentist's office*: Always be true
    to your teeth or they will be _____ to you.

16. *In a reducing salon*: A word to the _____
    is sufficient.

17. *In another health club*: Only 24 _____
    days 'til Christmas.

18. *In a body and fender repair shop*: May we have
    the next _____?

19. *In a florist's shop*: Light up your garden. Plant
    _____.

20. *In a garden shop*: We will sell no _____
    before its time.

If the English language made any sense, a teetotaler would be someone who counts golf pegs.
Senator Soaper

Poetic Licenses

On our nation's roads and highways you can find still more signs of the times. According to recent surveys, more than two million American motorists own vanity plates. Instead of getting stuck with meaningless, preselected letter-number combinations, more and more car owners are creating their own license plates. These *bon mot*orists use the five or six allotted letters and numbers to adorn their automobiles with succinct puns.

Reasons for owning a vanity license plate range from choosing a method of inexpensive and mobile advertising to communicating a message or expressing a sprightly sense of humor. Ah, vanity, vanity: all is vanity.

In the left-hand column below are fifteen authentic vanity license plates that have been recently registered with motor vehicle departments across the nation. Each plate announces, in a clever and compact way, the profession of the car owner. Match each plate in the left-hand column with the corresponding profession in the right-hand column.

RUREDY? GO4IT! Answers repose in the back of this book.

Example: A doctor's license plate reads YRUILL.

1. ADAM81   ____ aerobics instructor
2. BYLOW   ____ apple grower
3. CLUESO   ____ contractor
4. DECOR8   ____ dairy farmer
5. DOULIE   ____ dentist
6. 4CAST   ____ detective
7. IC2020   ____ eye doctor
8. IEDUC8   ____ interior decorator
9. IOPER8   ____ lawyer
10. ISUM4U   ____ police officer
11. LOCMUP   ____ polygraph examiner
12. MOOTEL   ____ school teacher
13. RENOV8   ____ stockbroker
14. 2THDR   ____ surgeon
15. YRUFAT   ____ weatherperson

Other personalized license plates convey a sense
of identity and humor, as illustrated by the authentic messages listed in the left-hand column below.
Match each plate with its creator, as listed in the
right-hand column.

16. DOIOU2   ____ Chicago Cubs fan
17. EIEIO   ____ farmer named McDonald
18. 4DCUBS   ____ flirt
19. HIOSVR   ____ habitual debtor
20. HIYAQT   ____ knitter
21. HOP2IT   ____ Lone Ranger fan
22. PURL2   ____ Miss Piggy fan
23. 2CTER   ____ sportscar owner
24. 10SNE1   ____ tennis buff
25. XQQMOI   ____ VW Rabbit owner

Playing around with the sounds of letters has
been a popular pastime in America, even before
automobiles and license plates appeared on the
scene. Here is a lovely example in verse by H.C.

Dodge that appeared in the July 1903 *Woman's Home Companion*. Have fun translating the poem.

> The farmer leads no EZ life.
>   The CD sows will rot;
> And when at EV rests from strife,
>   His bones will AK lot.
>
> In DD has to struggle hard
>   To EK living out;
> If IC frosts do not retard
>   His crops, there'll BA drought.
>
> The hired LP has to pay
>   Are awful AZ, too;
> They CK rest when he's away,
>   Nor NE work will do.
>
> Both NZ cannot make to meet,
>   And then for AD takes
> Some boarders, who so RT eat,
>   And E no money makes.
>
> Of little UC finds his life;
>   Sick in old AG lies;
> The debts he OZ leaves his wife,
>   And then in PC dies.

Let's continue to explore words that are letter perfect. Has it ever struck you that most of the letters in our alphabet sound like English words? To take four examples: *cue* and *queue* sound like the letter Q; *are* sounds like R; *ewe*, *you*, and *yew* sound like U; and *why* sounds like Y.

Here is a series of definitions, each of which yields a word that sounds just like a letter of the alphabet. Fill in each blank with the proper letter and then string the letters together to reveal the hidden message. If all your answers are correct, you'll reap a rich reward.

Answers to this puzzle and to the other letter perfect games that follow can be found in the answers section of this book.

1. a honey of an insect, exist ____

2. vision organ, pronoun ____

3. an exclamation ____

4. a blue and white bird ____

5. an indefinite article ____

6. A large body of water, to look ____

7. a woman's name ____

8. a green vegetable ____

9. to be in debt, an exclamation ____

10. a beverage, a golf peg ____

Each definition below yields a word that sounds just like the plural of a letter in the alphabet. Fill in the blanks with the correct words.

11. to grab ____

12. to make fun of ____

13. possessing wisdom ____

14. comfort ____

15. to utilize ____

Each definition below yields a word consisting entirely of letter sounds. The number of letters sounded in each word is represented by the parenthesized number.

Example: composition = essay (SA)

16. nothing inside (2) ____

17. not difficult (2) ____

18. wall-clinging plant (2) ____

19. jealousy (2) _____
20. slippery in winter (2) _____
21. to rot (2) _____
22. amusement park doll (2) _____
23. shrewd (2) _____
24. too much (2) _____
25. ocularly small and shiny (2) _____
26. shabby, run down (2) _____
27. award for best tv shows (2) _____
28. a foe (3) _____
29. title of high state official
    (4) _____
30. flower of the buttercup family
    (4) _____
31. one who leads a quiet and simple life
    (4) _____
32. convenience (5) _____

Finally, each clue below yields a proper name consisting entirely of letter sounds. The number of letters sounded in each name is represented by the parenthesized number.

33. He struck out. (2) _____
34. She's a contented cow. (2) _____
35. He's the dog in "Garfield." (2) _____
36. He used to lead Shaw's band. (2) _____
37. She started the Gibbs business schools.
    (2) _____
38. He courted an Irish Rose. (2) _____
39. He franchises roast beef. (2) _____
40. She was a Massachusetts poet. (3) _____

Trying to define humor is one of the definitions of humor.
Saul Steinberg

A Primer of Puns

A pun (in Greek, *paronomasia*, "equal word") has been defined as a play upun words and a bad pun as two-thirds of a pun—p.u. Such definitions do not satisfy the true investigator of language who is led to ask what is the nature of the word play and what is the nature of the words that are being played upon? To answer these questions, consider what the following examples of word finagling have in common:

- What did Samson die of?
  Fallen arches.

- What is six feet long, green, and has two tongues?
  The Jolly Green Giant's sneakers.

- Have you heard about the cannibal who had a wife and ate children?

- A matchup between two particularly inept football teams was called Game of the Weak.

- Bathing beauty: a girl worth wading for.

- Drunk drivers are people who put the quart before the hearse.

In each of these examples, two meanings, both related to the desired effect, are compacted within a single word. Each of the key words—*arches*,

tongues, *ate*, *Weak*, *wading*, *quart*, and *hearse*—
sparks forth multiple meanings or another spelling
or sound that invites additional interpretations.

Punnery is largely the trick of compacting two or
more ideas within a single word or expression. Punnery challenges us to apply the greatest pressure
per square syllable of language. Punnery surprises
us by flouting the law of nature that pretends that
two things cannot occupy the same space at the
same time. Punnery is an exercise of the mind at
being concise.

The more we play with words, the more we find
that most of them possess multiple meanings.
Because words are alive, they refuse to sit still. As
they grow older, they accumulate new meanings.
Words wander wondrously.

The most elemental and elementary form of punnery springs from a single word that generates two
or more different meanings. If those meanings are
founded on the same spelling, the pun is called a
homograph (Greek, "same writing").

Let's return to the first two examples in this
chapter:

- What did Samson die of?
  Fallen arches.

- What is six feet long, green, and has two
  tongues?
  The Jolly Green Giant's sneakers.

In the first riddle *arches* means both the curved
support of a building and the curved support of a
foot. In the second riddle, *tongues* are parts of
sneakers and parts of mouths.

Here are five graphic homographs created by
famous people:

- *Cicero*: (of a farmer who had plowed up the field where his father was buried) This is truly to cultivate a father's memory.

- *Sir Walter Scott*: Please return my book. I find that though many of my friends are poor arithmeticians, they are nearly all good bookkeepers.

- *Benjamin Franklin*: (during the signing of the Declaration of Independence) We must all hang together or, most assuredly, we shall hang separately.

- *Edgar Bergen and/or Charlie McCarthy*: Show me where Stalin is buried and I'll show you a communist plot.

- *Ronald Reagan*: (during arms talks with Mikhail Gorbachev) It was a proposal, one might say, disarmingly simple.

Now let's get a little more complex. If, in the word play, the spelling differs according to each meaning, we have a homophone pun (Greek, "same sound"). Let's review the third and fourth examples that started this chapter:

- Have you heard about the cannibal who had a wife and ate children?

- A matchup between two particularly inept football teams was called Game of the Weak.

In this pair, *ate* is the past tense of *eat*, but its sound suggests another spelling, *eight*, a number, while *Weak*, "inept," spawns *Week*, "seven days."

Many English speaking children have recited a version of this rhyme:

How much wood would a woodchuck chuck
If a woodchuck could chuck wood?

A woodchuck would chuck
All the wood that a woodchuck could chuck
If a woodchuck could chuck wood.

The delight and popularity of this little verse can be explained by the lively rhythms, the clever rhyming of *woodchuck* and *could chuck*, and the homographic pun on *woodchuck* and *would chuck*.

Perhaps the most popular of all children's riddles is: What's black and white and red (read) all over? – a newspaper. Again we have a homophone, with its play on *red* and *read*. Taking flight from the first meaning, more recent answers include:

- A penguin at Miami Beach.
- A zebra with diaper rash.
- A skunk with the measles.
- A nun who's spilled ketchup on herself.
- Santa Claus coming down the chimney.
- *Pravda*.

The canon of the single sound pun has fired off some remarkably high caliber boomers. Here are some triple plays as rare and flashy as Halley's Comet:

- A man gave his sons a cattle ranch and named it Focus because it was a spot where the sons raise meat.
- Pharaoh's daughter was like a stock broker because she took a little prophet from the rushes on the banks.
- Television is like a steak: a medium rarely well done.

What may be the most compacted of all single sound puns is this astonishing sextuple play: Charlemagne mustered his Francs to assault and pepper the Saracens with great relish, but he couldn't catch up. (Frankly, I never sausage a pun. It's the wurst!)

Now return one last time to the six examples that head this chapter. How do the last two differ from the others?

- Bathing beauty: a girl worth wading for.

- Drunk drivers are people who put the quart before the hearse.

In homograph and homophone puns, one sound yields two or more meanings. In the two examples we are considering, a slightly more complex process is at work. One sound generates two meanings, but the second meaning comes through a second sound phonetically related to the original sound. Thus *wading*, "stepping through water," suggests *waiting*, "expecting," and *quart*, "a measure," and *hearse*, "a carrier at a funeral," suggest *cart*, "a small wagon," and *horse*, "an animal." This kind of phonetic finagling makes double sound puns.

The title of this book is a double sound pun. *Get Thee To a Punnery* calls up Hamlet's angry advice to Ophelia: "Get thee to a nunnery," which itself is a homograph pun on the two meanings of *nunnery* that existed in Elizabethan slang, "a place where nuns live" and "a bawdy house" — or, as Archie Bunker once called it, "a house of ill refute."

Here are five dazzling double sound puns emitted by the illuminati:

- *Oliver Wendell Holmes*: As a physician, I am grateful for small fevers.

- *George S. Kaufman*: One man's Mede is another man's Persian.

- *Groucho Marx*: When shooting elephants in

Africa, I found the tusks very difficult to remove, but in Alabama the Tuscaloosa.

- *Peter De Vries*: The things my wife buys at auctions are keeping me baroque.

- *Fred Allen*: Hanging is too good for a man who makes puns. He ought to be drawn and quoted.

I'm confident that you are now prepared for the quizzes on single and double sound puns that I'm about to pop on you in the upcoming chapters. Later in this book, I'll cover two additional types of punnery — meld puns and spoonerisms.

The main idea to hold in mind is that, as varied as these methods are, they all have one thing in common. In every example two or more meanings are packed into a verbal space that they do not occupy in ordinary discourse.

The fact that people and trees and elephants and cars all have trunks just proves that there are more things than there are words.

Scot Morris

Homographs:
The Antics of Semantics

The notorious punster, Thomas Hood, wrote in "Faithless Nelly Gray":

> Ben Battle was a soldier bold,
> And used to war's alarms;
> But a cannon ball took off his legs,
> So he laid down his arms.

From behind his quatrain Hood winks at us by playing on the double meaning of *arms* — "limbs" and "weapons" — a literary example of homographic word play.

To sharpen your awareness of multiple meanings springing from a single spelling, try your hand and imagination at playing three games of homography. All answers repose in the back of this book.

As the quotation at the top of this page implies, to a doctor, a trunk is a human torso; to a forester, a trunk is the main support of a tree; to a zoo keeper, a trunk is an elephant's appendage; and to a car owner, a trunk is a space for storage.

In each cluster of sentences below, identify the single word that can occupy each blank:

1. To a jeweler, a _____ is a round band.

   To someone answering the phone, a _____ is an audible signal.

   To a boxer, a _____ is an enclosure to fight in.

   To an astronomer, a _____ is a circle of matter surrounding a heavenly body.

2. To most of us, a _____ is something at the end of our arm.

   To a ship's captain, a _____ is a crew member.

   To a card player, a _____ is a collection or round of cards.

   To an entertainer, a _____ is a round of applause.

   To a clockmaker, a _____ is a pointer on a dial.

   To a calligrapher, a _____ is a style of writing.

   To a horse trainer, a _____ is a measurement of height.

3. To a collector, a _____ is a number of things of the same kind.

   To a director, a _____ is the scene for a production.

   To a beautician, a _____ is an arrangement of hair.

   To a musician, a _____ is a session of music.

   To a bridge player, a _____ is the defeat of a contract.

To a tennis player, a _____ is a portion of a match.

4. To most of us, the _____ are a bad case of the blahs.

To a musician, the _____ is a kind of jazz.

To an architect, the _____ are preliminary diagrams.

To a Civil War buff, the _____ are Union soldiers.

To a person concerned with health care, the _____ are Blue Cross and Blue Shield.

5. To an employer, a _____ is a work stoppage.

To a bowler, a _____ is knocking down all ten pins.

To a baseball player, a _____ is a missed pitch.

To a fisherman, a _____ is a pull on the line.

To a prospector, a _____ is a valuable discovery.

To a producer, a _____ is taking down a set.

To a soldier, a _____ is an attack.

To strengthen your grasp of homographic arts, I offer another game. In each blank below insert a word that means the same as the two words or phrases that come before and after. The dashes indicate the number of letters in each missing word.

6. summit ___ ___ ___ spinning toy

7. dance ___ ___ ___ ___ spheroid

8. gasps ___ ___ ___ ___ ___ trousers

9. remainder __ __ __ __ relaxation

10. throw __ __ __ __ __ tar

11. close __ __ __ __ sea lion

12. plunge __ __ __ __ season

13. ignite __ __ __ __ release from job

14. hole __ __ __ fruit stone

15. coil __ __ __ __ __ __ running water

16. playing area __ __ __ __ __ hall of justice

17. gravesite __ __ __ __ scheme

18. without cost __ __ __ __ liberate

19. contest __ __ __ __ __ fire stick

20. nation __ __ __ __ __ __ __ rural area

21. cliff __ __ __ __ deception

22. food __ __ __ __ __ plank

23. alteration __ __ __ __ __ coins

24. whip __ __ __ __ part of eye

25. student __ __ __ __ __ part of eye

26. vessel __ __ __ __ __ __ __ hurler

27. post __ __ __ __ __ bet

28. run __ __ __ __ hyphen

29. beak __ __ __ __ charge

30. layer __ __ __ __ outer garment

31. card __ __ __ expert

32. dead heat __ __ __ article of clothing

33. sovereign __ __ __ __ __ measuring device

34. disc __ __ __ __ __ __ achievement

35. illustrate __ __ __ __ extract

36. blockage __ __ __ jelly

37. dash __ __ __ __ projectile

38. rubbish __ __ __ __ __ __ newborn animals

39. flavor __ __ __ __ money factory

40. rub smooth __ __ __ __ arrange

The vocabulary of the English language contains anywhere from 750,000 to one million words — by far the largest in the history of humankind. Despite this impressive achievement, many words in English have to do double duty and convey more than one meaning.

Here's an illustration. What is the opposite of the word *heavy*? Most likely, you answered *light*. Now, what is the opposite of the word *dark*? Again you probably answered *light*. Because *light* has at least two meanings, it functions as the opposite of two very different words.

To uncover more double duty homographs, try playing the following game. Fill in each blank with a word that is opposite to the word listed on the left and to the different word listed on the right.

41. loud _____ hard

42. young _____ new

43. wrong _____ left

44. tall _____ long

45. smooth _____ gentle

46. even _____ normal

47. sharp _____ interesting

48. costly _____ enslaved

49. bring _____ give

50. rich _____ excellent

51. happy _____ sane

52. win _____ find

53. soft _____ easy

54. past _____ absent
55. foul _____ dark
56. stop _____ come
57. multiple _____ married
58. good _____ healthy
59. major _____ adult
60. common _____ well done
61. coarse _____ sick
62. loose _____ slow
63. stale _____ polite
64. unbiased _____ complete
65. front _____ forth

A pun's the lowest form of wit,
It does not tax the brain a bit;
One merely takes a word that's
   plain
And picks one out that sounds
   the same.

Anonymous

Homophones:
What Do You Call
a Naked Grizzly?

There was a young girl, a sweet lamb,
Who smiled as she entered a tram.
   After she had embarked,
   The conductor remarked,
"Your fare." And she blushed, "Yes, I am."

This little verse was written by that prolific Irish limericist Ann O'Nymous. The humor of the story plays on the identical sounds but multiple meanings of the words *your* and *you're* and *fare* and *fair*. As you know, words that sound alike but are spelled differently and have different meanings are called homophones.

Here is a game designed to open your eyes and ears to the joys of homophony. Each of the following clues should lead you to a phrase consisting of two homophones. The first twenty-seven answers involve the animal kingdom. All solutions are in the answer section of this book.

Example: A naked grizzly is a *bare bear*.

1. female deer sleep _____ _____
2. raspy throated equine _____ _____
3. insect relative _____ _____
4. tiresome pig _____ _____
5. cry from the largest mammal _____ _____
6. rabbit fur _____ _____
7. stinking chicken _____ _____
8. fighting ape _____ _____
9. precious buck _____ _____
10. antlered animal's dessert _____ _____
11. dragged cousin of the frog _____ _____
12. inexpensive chick's cry _____ _____
13. wildcat's chain parts _____ _____
14. smoked salmon fastenings _____ _____
15. mollusk brawn _____ _____
16. horrible bear _____ _____
17. runs from insects _____ _____
18. donkey whimper _____ _____
19. recently acquired antelope _____ _____
20. female sheep utilize _____ _____
21. animal feet stop _____ _____
22. line of fish eggs _____ _____
23. flock listened _____ _____
24. appendage story _____ _____
25. small insect power _____ _____

26. buy bird stations _____ _____

27. encounter animal flesh _____ _____

28. wan bucket _____ _____

29. double sword fight _____ _____

30. dungarees for chromosomes _____ _____

31. basement salesperson _____ _____

32. sugary collection of rooms _____ _____

33. change the worship platform _____ _____

34. corridor on an island _____ _____

35. unadorned airliner _____ _____

36. forbidden music group _____ _____

37. ostracized poet _____ _____

38. rapier flew _____ _____

39. correct ceremony _____ _____

40. young coal digger _____ _____

41. villainous singer _____ _____

42. to taunt golf pegs _____ _____

43. to inveigle soft drinks _____ _____

44. hurled royal chair _____ _____

45. entire burrow _____ _____

46. spun globe _____ _____

47. boat canvas bargains _____ _____

48. visitor estimated _____ _____

49. braver rock _____ _____

50. ground grain blossom _____ _____

51. tube to wash garden tools _____ _____

52. fearful man quivered _____ _____

53. rogue's section of a church _____ _____

54. large frame _____ _____

55. rowing team's ship tour _____ _____
56. inactive false god _____ _____
57. cuts back classes _____ _____
58. mansion's etiquette _____ _____
59. conceited blood channel _____ _____
60. main code of conduct _____ _____
61. prognosticator's gain _____ _____
62. stick for roasting beef _____ _____
63. odd market place _____ _____
64. what a foot doctor does _____ _____
65. peels fruit _____ _____
66. sabbath ice cream treat _____ _____
67. two played, but only _____ _____
68. rough track _____ _____
69. grieving at dawn _____ _____
70. window glass agony _____ _____
71. officer's seeds _____ _____
72. levy on push nails _____ _____
73. male float _____ _____
74. masculine postal items _____ _____
75. king's son's reproductions _____ _____
76. singing skeletal deposits _____ _____
77. kills sleds _____ _____
78. corny labyrinth _____ _____
79. sedentary writing paper _____ _____
80. military belly button _____ _____
81. medieval darkness _____ _____
82. gathered the condiment _____ _____
83. single animating essence _____ _____

84. perceives the deep waters _____ _____
85. octet consumed food _____ _____
86. boarder gossip _____ _____
87. uninterested plank _____ _____
88. renter's boundary _____ _____
89. lift sunbeams _____ _____
90. solar offsprings _____ _____
91. Scandinavian ending _____ _____
92. roped incoming ocean _____ _____
93. untruthful stringed instrument _____ _____
94. convalescent's forbearance _____ _____
95. penny perfume _____ _____
96. listen on this spot _____ _____
97. more disgusting food seller _____ _____
98. more skillful wager _____ _____
99. grape alcohol lament _____ _____
100. catcalls for alcohol _____ _____

> *Knock, knock, knock. Who's there i' th' name of Belzebub? . . . Knock, knock. Who's there, in th' other devil's name? . . . Knock, knock, knock. Who's there? Never at quiet!*
>
> William Shakespeare
> *Macbeth*, Act 2, Scene 3

Double Sound Puns: Don't Knock Knock-Knock Jokes

Knock, knock.
Who's there?
Hearsay.
Hearsay who?
Hearsay chapter of knock-knock jokes.

It may be stretching a point (Knock, knock . . . Who's there? A point . . . A point who? . . . A point is half a quart) to assert that Shakespeare (Shakespeare who? Shakesperience is the best teacher) invented the knock-knock joke, but the genre has been popular since the 1920s.

Paul Dickson believes that "the knock-knock may be the first truly American formulaic form of humor," one that has become an integral part of American folk culture. Most of us play the game as children, and many of us continue knock-knocking right through adulthood.

The jokester says, "Knock, knock." The second person replies, "Who's there?" The knock-knocker comes back with something like "Dwayne." "Dwayne who?" is the ritual response. Then the punch line perpetrates a preposterous, and almost always double sound, pun, such as "Dwayne the bathtub; I'm dwowning."

> Knock, knock.
> Who's there?
> Hair comb.
> Hair comb who?
> Hair comb two games of knock-knock jokes.

The first quiz plays upon people's names. Match each name in the list below with the appropriate conclusion that follows. You can open the door to all answers in this chapter by turning to the back pages.

Knock, knock. Who's there? . . .

Adelle	Eisenhower	José	Sam and Janet
Amos	Freda	Keith	Sarah
Andy	Harry	Lionel	Sherwood
Arthur	Henrietta	Nicholas	Tarzan
Barry	Humphrey	Oliver	Theresa
Ben Hur	Ira	Osborn	Walter
Della	Isabel	Oswald	Wayne
Desdemona	Isadore	Phillip	Wendy
Dexter	Ivan	Raleigh	Yoda

(Name) Who?

1. _____ can you see?
2. _____ big dinner and got sick.

3. _____ dwops keep falling on my head.

4. _____ stripes forever.

5. _____ my bubble gum.

6. _____ catessen.

7. _____ is what a farmer lives in.

8. _____ 'round the flag, boys.

9. _____ locked?

10. _____ half as much as a dime.

11. _____ in the USA.

12. _____ quito bit me.

13. _____ bit me again.

14. _____ to be alone.

15. _____ wall carpeting.

16. _____ moon comes over the mountain.

17. _____ halls with boughs of holly.

18. _____ roar if you don't feed it.

19. _____ like a cold drink.

20. _____ me not on the lone prairie.

21. _____ prisoners.

22. _____ the tub so I can take a bath.

23. _____ green, except in winter.

24. _____ an hour, and she hasn't shown up.

25. _____ up, we're late.

26. _____ troubles will soon be over.

27. _____ late for work.

28. _____ doctor in the house?

29. _____ mometer is broken.

30. _____ member Mama.

31. _____ out of order?

32. _____ Lisa hanging on the wall.

33. _____ ever blowing bubbles.

34. _____ evening, you may see a stranger.

35. _____ me, pleath.

36. _____ best knock-knock jokester I've met.

Knock, knock.
Who's there?
Samoa.
Samoa who?
Samoa knock-knock jokes are about to come your way.

This second game plays upon words other than people's names. Match each word in the list below with the appropriate conclusion that follows.

Knock, knock. Who's there? . . .

aardvark	cheetahs	hyena	omelette
ammonia	cirrhosis	ketchup	ooze
amoeba	despair	kleenex	pecan
avenue	doughnut	lilac	radio
baloney	effervescent	llama	sofa
bay	event	macho	tequila
canoe	eyewash	manor	toucan
catgut	fangs	meretricious	tuba
censure	hence	needle	zombies

(Word) Who?

37. _____ lay eggs.

38. _____ toothpaste.

39. _____ so good.

40. _____ are prettier than dirty necks.

41. _____ to her before she gets away.

42. _____ make honey, and _____ don't.

43. _____ smarter than I look.

44. _____ dumb, but I'm not crazy.

45. _____ a rug.

46. _____ live as cheaply as one.

47. _____ not, here I come!

48. _____ mockingbird.

49. _____ afraid of the big, bad wolf?

50. _____ help me with my homework?

51. _____ open until Christmas.

52. _____ you a Merry Christmas.

53. _____ and a happy New Year.

54. _____ never prosper.

55. _____ for the memories.

56. _____ is the key to success.

57. _____ by face, I love your pretty, little _____ by face.

58. _____ tire is flat.

59. _____ Yankee Doodle Dandy.

60. _____ thataway!

61. _____ for television, I'd be bored.

62. _____ do about nothing.

63. _____ your tongue?

64. _____ tree sat an owl.

65. _____ red and the violet is blue.

66. _____ somebody your own size.

67. _____ little money for the movies?

68. _____ so smart, why aren't you rich?

69. _____ bird in a silver cage.

70. _____ God can make a tree.

71. _____ mouse – which one are you?

72. _____ heard these jokes before?

Knock, knock. Who's there? Arthur. Arthur who? Arthur any more knock-knock jokes?

Yes, hundreds. But . . . Knock, knock. Who's there? Celeste. Celeste who? Celeste chance I have to inflict more knock-knock jokes on you.

Knock, knock. Who's there? Orange juice. Orange juice who? Orange juice glad I'm nearing the end of this chapter?

Knock, knock. Who's there? Amsterdam. Amsterdam who? Amsterdam tired of these infernal knock-knock jokes.

Knock, knock. Who's there? Consumption. Consumption who? Consumption be done about idiots who keep telling knock-knock jokes?

Knock, knock. Who's there? Apostle. Apostle who? Apostle of outraged readers armed with blackjacks and brass knuckles who have come to trash any jokester who persists in playing this foolish knock-knock game.

Knock, knock . . .

> On the making of puns: *One must strike while the irony is hot.*
>
> Phyllis McGinley

Punupmanship

H ave you ever wondered how we got the expression *funny bone*? Technically it is the ulnar nerve that causes that tingly sensation when we strike our arm, but the source of that feeling is the enlarged knob on the end of the bone running from the shoulder to the elbow. The medical name for that particular bone is the humerus, and back in 1840 some wag seized upon the homophonic similarity of *humerus* and *humorous* and dubbed the humerus the funny bone, a learned pun that has become part of our language.

Now that you've struck your funny bone on homographs, homophones, and double sound puns, I offer a three-part test designed to solidify and measure your skills in punupmanship. Do not look at the answers in the back of the book until you have completed the entire test.

Scoring

90–100 — Master punster

80–89 — Proficient pundit

60–79 — Promising punhead

0–59 — Pundemonium!

Enjoy the remaining games in this book. Then try the test in the last chapter.

Part I

Label each of the puns below as homographic, homophonic, or double sound.

HOMOGRAPHIC HOMOPHONIC DOUBLE SOUND

1. ☐ ☐ ☐ Queen Elizabeth I, who had an age named after her, quipped to one of her noblemen, "You may be burly, my Lord of Burleigh, but ye shall make less stir in my realm than the Lord of Leicester."

2. ☐ ☐ ☐ King Charles I once asked his jester to make a pun. "Upon what subject?" asked the fool. "Make one on me," said Charles. "But that I cannot do," responded the jester, "for the king is no subject."

3. ☐ ☐ ☐ Here's how to make a fortune. Buy fifty female pigs and fifty male deer. Then you'll have a hundred sows and bucks.

4. ☐ ☐ ☐ Sometimes parents pay $80,000 to put their son through college, and all they get is a quarterback.

5. ☐ ☐ ☐ What's the difference between the Prince of Wales, an ape, and a bald-headed man? The Prince of Wales is the heir apparent, an ape has a hairy parent, and a bald-headed man has no hair apparent.

6. ☐ ☐ ☐ In what direction does a sneeze usually travel? Atchoo!

HOMOGRAPHIC HOMOPHONIC DOUBLE SOUND

7. ☐ ☐ ☐ Have you heard about the butcher who backed into the meat grinder? He got a little behind in his work.

8. ☐ ☐ ☐ Have you heard about the dragon bully who didn't observe the Sabbath? He only preyed on weak knights.

9. ☐ ☐ ☐ How do you mend a broken heart? With ticker tape.

10. ☐ ☐ ☐ When a musician left his saxophone and violins on top of the television set, his wife complained that there was too much sax and violins on television.

11. ☐ ☐ ☐ The Brontë sisters all wrote novels and poems. They were engaged in a scribbling rivalry.

12. ☐ ☐ ☐ An anarchist was out walking in the country with a bomb secreted under his trenchcoat. Seeing another man coming down the road his way, the anarchist chucked the bomb into a nearby pasture and fled. A bull approached the bomb and swallowed it. Summarize the result in a single word. Abominable.

13. ☐ ☐ ☐ Two ropes entered a restaurant. The waiter asked the first rope, "Are you one of them ropes?" "Why, yes," stammered the rope. "We

HOMOGRAPHIC HOMOPHONIC DOUBLE SOUND

don't serve your kind," spat the waiter and whirled the rope around in the air and threw him out the window and into the street.

The second rope decided that he'd better disguise himself, so he made his two ends all raggedy and curled himself into a knot. Then the waiter walked up to him and asked, "Are you one of them ropes?"

Replied the rope: "I'm a frayed knot."

14. ☐ ☐ ☐ Twice a year we reset our clocks and watches according to the mnemonic adage "Fall back; spring ahead."

15. ☐ ☐ ☐ Quiche me — I'm French.

16. ☐ ☐ ☐ She was only an optician's daughter, but she really made a spectacle of herself.

17. ☐ ☐ ☐ She was only a stableman's daughter, but all the horsemen knew her.

18. ☐ ☐ ☐ Wintertime is the age of shivery and shovelry.

19. ☐ ☐ ☐ Missionary to natives: "Do you practice cannibalism?" Answer: "No, we're already very good at it."

20. ☐ ☐ ☐ When someone exultantly exclaimed "Eureka!" Chico Marx shot back, "You donna smella so good youself!"

HOMOGRAPHIC HOMOPHONIC DOUBLE SOUND

21. ☐ ☐ ☐ One day Mr. Snail decided to buy a snappy sports car. To add distinction, Snail asked the salesman to paint a large *S* on the hood, trunk, and all sides. "Driving fast is a real ego trip," said Snail. "Now everyone who sees me will say, 'Look at the *S* car go!' "

22. ☐ ☐ ☐ The Yiddish comedian had oi vay with words and always earned a standing oi vay-tion.

23. ☐ ☐ ☐ Knock, knock. Who's there? Electrolux. Electrolux who? Electrolux her father but hates her mother.— Triinu Mikiver

24. ☐ ☐ ☐ Zsa Zsa Gabor once observed: "I am a very good housekeeper. Each time I get divorced I keep the house."

25. ☐ ☐ ☐ When Dorothy Parker was challenged to use the word *horticulture* in a sentence, she promptly replied, "You can lead a horticulture, but you can't make her think."

In his cynic's lexicon, *The Devil's Dictionary*, Ambrose Bierce defined *helpmate* as "wife, the bitter half." Label each of the following devilish definitions as homographic, homophonic, or double sound.

26. ☐ ☐ ☐ *alarm clock.* A device designed to scare the daylights out of you.

HOMOGRAPHIC HOMOPHONIC DOUBLE SOUND

27. ☐ ☐ ☐ *archaeologist*. A man whose career lies in ruins.

28. ☐ ☐ ☐ *committee*. A group of men who keep minutes and waste hours. — Milton Berle

29. ☐ ☐ ☐ *diplomacy*. Lying in state. — Oliver Herford

30. ☐ ☐ ☐ *diplomat*. One who can be disarming, even if his country isn't.

31. ☐ ☐ ☐ *egotist*. One who is me-deep in conversation.

32. ☐ ☐ ☐ *flattery*. Phony express. — John Wayne

33. ☐ ☐ ☐ *gossip*. A person with a keen sense of rumor.

34. ☐ ☐ ☐ *husband*. What is left over after the nerve has been extracted. — Helen Rowland

35. ☐ ☐ ☐ *income tax*. Capital punishment.

36. ☐ ☐ ☐ *kleptomaniac*. One who can't help himself from helping himself. — Henry Morgan

37. ☐ ☐ ☐ *middle age*. When actions creak louder than words.

38. ☐ ☐ ☐ *plea bargaining*. Using a proposition to end a sentence with.

39. ☐ ☐ ☐ *saxophone*. An ill wind nobody blows any good.

40. ☐ ☐ ☐ *world*. A puzzle with a peace missing.

Part II

Use the puns in the list below to complete each statement that follows.

Abyssinia	habit	mare
amnesia	heir	marmalade
anemones	hippo	Omar Khayyam
baited	hoe, hoe, hoe	pucker
buoy	hole	rhyme
circuit	inhibited	saucers
cremated	Juvenal	sheikh
Eumenides	leaving	smoting
Euripides	line	threw
grab	linoleum	towed

41. Midget wrestlers travel around the country on the short _____.

42. Shoplifters are cursed with the gift of _____.

43. With fronds like this, who needs _____?

44. A baker quit making doughnuts because he got tired of the _____ business.

45. A knight decided to throw away his sword and shield and give up _____ for good. – Alan Sherman

46. The frustrated golfer drove over the river and _____ the woods. – Eric S. Hansen

47. The best remedy for forgetfulness is milk of _____.

48. A nun got her skirt caught in a revolving door, so she entered the building by force of _____.

49. People who worry a lot about their weight could be called _____ chondriacs.

50. Sir Lancelot's horse was a knight _____.

51. Romance on the ocean: Gull meets _____.

52. What do you get when you roll a hand grenade across a kitchen floor? _____ blownapart. – Amy Ensign.

53. How do you kiss a hockey player? You _____ up.

54. What does Santa Claus do in his three gardens? _____.

55. Many a poet has learned that _____ doesn't pay.

56. Upon discovering a new egg in the henhouse, the excited chick chirped, "_____ a baby!"

57. When carrier doves deliver the mail, we can say that the letters are pigeon-_____.

58. A whale swallowed some worms in order to lure fish into his mouth. Then he waited for the fish with _____ breath.

59. A man who angers his wife is likely to encounter flying _____.

60. Alimony is the high cost of _____.

61. One of the advantages of nuclear warfare is that all men are _____ equal. – Max Eastman

62. What did the tailor say when the Greek trage-dian handed him a pair of trousers? "_____?"

63. "Yes," replied the tragedian. "_____?"

64. Why did the hen cross to the middle of the road? She wanted to lay it on the _____.

65. One day the sultan unexpectedly paid a visit to his harem and let out a terrified _____.

66. When Antony asked Cleopatra if she was in love with him, she responded, "_____!"

67. A Latin student flunked a course because of _____ delinquency.

68. In ancient times people had little need of psychiatrists because the country was sparsely _____.

69. The man who changed his will every week became a fresh _____ fiend.

70. So long, _____.

Part III

Now you are entirely on your own. I provide no clues to help you figure out the pun or puns necessary to complete each statement below. But I'm confident that you won't draw too many blanks in filling in the blanks.

71. Out on the ocean a ship carrying red paint crashed into another ship carrying blue paint. What happened to the crews? They all got _____.

72. What happened when the cow tried to jump over the barbed wire fence? _____ disaster.

73. A decrepit old gas man named Peter,
    While hunting around for the meter,
        Struck a leak with his light:
        He was blown out of sight,
    And, as anyone can see by reading this limerick,
    he also destroyed the _____.

74. A tutor who tooted the flute
    Tried to tutor two tooters to toot.
       Said the two to the tutor,
       "Is it easier to _____ or
    To tutor two tooters to toot?"

75. Back-straighteners in Egypt are called _____ practors.

76. I'm on a seafood diet. Every time I _____ food, I eat it.

77. A woman in the dentist's chair refused to be given Novocain because she wanted to transcend dental _____.

78. When the glassblower accidently inhaled, he ended up with a _____ in his stomach.

79. A headmaster adored all the students in his school. One day, masons laid down a cement pathway leading to his house, and some of the young scholars ran across the path before it was dry. Angered, the headmaster beat the boys unmercifully. Apparently he loved children in the abstract, but not in the _____.

80. An igloo is an _____ built for two.

81. What do you call an empty frankfurter? A hollow _____.

82. What is the richest country in the world? Ireland, because its capital is always _____.

83. Truth in advertising laws have taken the wind out of a lot of people's _____.

84. The only duck ever to be elected an American president was _____ Fillmore.

85. The elephants went on strike because they got tired of working for _____.

86. Who were the three most constipated men in the Bible? Cain because he wasn't _____. Methuselah because he sat on the _____ for 900 years. And Moses because God gave him two _____ and sent him into the wilderness.

87. Why didn't they play cards on Noah's Ark? Because Noah sat on the _____.

88. Why weren't there any worms on Noah's Ark? Because worms come in apples, not in _____.

89. Bumper sticker: _____, _____, so off to work I go.

90. Have you heard about the new restaurant on the moon? The food is great, but it just doesn't have any _____.

91. A monastery was famous for its delicious fish and chips. The chief cooks were the fish _____ and the chip _____.

92. When his parachute failed to open, the paratrooper found himself jumping to a _____.

93. My parents are in the iron and steel business. My mother irons, and my father _____.

94. What is the favorite part of a highway for a vampire? The main _____.

95. The only man who always got his work done by _____ was Robinson Crusoe.

96. What do you get when you cross a cantaloupe and Lassie? A _____ baby.

97. When I am dead, I hope it may be said:
'His sins were scarlet,
But his books were _____.'
                               – Hilaire Belloc

98. The sum total of the national debt is _____ total.

99. Aging rabbis tend to get gray around the _____.

100. The inept music critic just didn't know his brass from his _____.

A pun is language on vacation.
Christopher Morley

Have You Ever Seen a Horse Fly?

W hat is wrong with each of these newspaper headlines?:

TEACHER STRIKES IDLE KIDS

CYPRUS FIGHTING MUSHROOMS

EYE DROPS OFF SHELF

SQUAD HELPS DOG BITE VICTIM

BRITISH LEFT WAFFLES ON FALKLANDS

In each case the headline can be read two ways because of a confusion in the part of speech of one or more of its words, thus generating an inadvertent pun.

The ability of many English words to rail jump from one part of speech to another is called conversion or function shift. This lively characteristic of our language has produced not only a number of two-headed headlines, but also a bookful of riddles:

- What has four wheels and flies? *A garbage truck.*

- How do you make an elephant stew? *Keep it waiting for two hours.*

- What makes the Tower of Pisa lean? *It never eats.*
- How can you make money fast? *Don't feed it.*
- What did Silly Billy do when he came to a gas station with a sign that said "Clean Rest Rooms"? *He went inside and cleaned them.*

The easy interchangeability of nouns and verbs in English has inspired a little game called "Have you ever seen?"

Have you ever seen . . .

- a horse fly?
- a ski jump?
- a vegetable stand?
- a board walk?
- a jelly roll?
- an antique shop?
- a rock star?
- a mouse trap?
- a turkey shoot?

In each joke the pun shuttles back and forth between noun and verb.

Now it's your turn to play the game. Match the words in the left-hand column with the appropriate words in the right-hand column. Compare your answers with those in the back of the book.

Have you ever seen . . .

1. a ball _____   bowl?
2. a bell _____   box?
3. a belly _____   bud? garden?
4. a bull _____   call? fish? nap? nip?
5. a cat _____   chop?

6. a chair _____   clown?

7. a chimney _____   cut?

8. a circus _____   dance?

9. an egg _____   deal?

10. a fox _____   duck?

11. a garden _____   fence?

12. a ginger _____   flop? laugh?

13. a hack _____   hop?

14. a hair _____   hunt? trot?

15. a home _____   lift?

16. a key _____   park?

17. a kitchen _____   party?

18. a lamb _____   plant? roll? shampoo?

19. a package _____   punch? ring?

20. a peppermint _____ run?

21. a picket _____   rush? whip?

22. a roast _____   saw?

23. a rose _____   shovel? storm?

24. a salad _____   sink?

25. a shoe _____   snap?

26. a snow _____   sweep?

27. a square _____   twist?

28. a toy _____   whistle?

> *Never point a pun at a friend. It might be loaded. Besides, you might kill a pun pal.*
>
> John Crosbie

Four Cheers Five Inflationary Language

Many years ago, the pianist and comedian Victor Borge popularized the game of inflationary language. Since prices keep going up, Borge reasoned, why shouldn't language go up, too.

In the English language there are words that contain the sounds of numbers, like *wonder*, *before*, and *decorate*. If we inflate each sound by one, we come up with a string of single sound puns — *twoder*, *befive*, and *decornine*.

I have adapted Borge's idea in the story that follows, a tale that invites you to read and hear inflationary language in all its inflated grandeur. Try your eye and ear at translating the text back into regular, uninflated English. Then check your results with the translation that appears in the back of this book.

Jack and the Twoderful Beans

Twice upon a time there lived a boy named Jack in the twoderful land of Califivenia. Two day Jack, a double-minded lad, decided three go fifth three seek his fivetune.

After making sure that Jack nine a sandwich and drank some Eight-Up and quiten, his mother elevenderly said, "Threedeloo, threedeloo. Try three be back by next Threesday." Then she cheered, "Three-five-seven-nine. Who do we apprecinine? Jack, Jack, yay!"

Jack set fifth and soon met a man wearing a four-piece suit and a threepee. Fifthrightly Jack asked the man, "I'm a Califivenian. Are you two three?"

"Cerelevenly," replied the man, offiving the high six. "Anytwo five elevennis?"

"Not threeday," answered Jack inelevently. "But can you help me three locnine my fivetune?"

"Sure," said the man. "Let me sell you these twoderful beans."

Jack's inthreeition told him that the man was a three-faced triple-crosser. Elevensely Jack shouted, "You must think I'm an asiten idiot who's behind the nine ball. But I'm a college gradunine, and I know what rights our fivefathers crenined in the Constithreetion. Now let's get down three baseven about these beans. If you're intoxicnined, I'll never fivegive you!"

The man tripled over with laughter. "Now hold on a third," he responded. "There's no need three make such an unfivetunine three-do about these beans. It's seven of two and half of thirteen of the other three me, but you won't find twoderful beans like this at the Eight Twelve."

Jack pulled out his trusty seven-shooter and exclaimed, "I'll make you change out of that four-piece suit and wear a threethree. Then I'll blow you three Timbukthree!" Jack then shot off the man's threepee. "Go away and recupernine at the Esseven Hospital. But second I twot you three give me the beans."

Well, there's no need three elabornine on the rest of the tale. Jack elevenaciously oned in on the giant and two the battle for the golden eggs. He eliminined the big guy, and Jack and his mother were in eighth heaven and on cloud ten fivever after—and so on, and so on, and so fifth.

*I calls out: The door has twinges
and a pane, and it's in a jamb. 'O
pun!' he sesame.*

Sara Young

'Let's Play a Game,'
Said Tom Swiftly

During the early part of this century, boys and girls grew up devouring the adventures of Tom Swift, a sterling young hero created by Edward Stratemeyer. In Stratemeyer's stories, Tom and his friends and enemies never just said something: they always said it *excitedly* or *sadly* or *hurriedly*.

Tom Swift and his wonderful electric aeroplane have been mothballed, but the adverbial pun game known as Tom Swifties still flies. The object is to match the adverb with the quotation to produce, in each case, a high-flying pun:

- "I love pancakes," said Tom flippantly.
- "My pants are wrinkled," said Tom ironically.
- "I've run out of laundry detergent," said Tom cheerlessly.
- "I hate pineapples," said Tom dolefully.
- "The stock market's going up," said Tom bullishly.
- "This isn't real turtle soup," said Tom mockingly.
- "Brew me more coffee," said Tom perkily.

- "You're a real zero," said Tom naughtily.
- "No, Eve, I won't touch that apple," said Tom adamantly.
- "My favorite statue is the Venus de Milo," said Tom disarmingly.
- "Let's go to McDonald's," said Tom archly.
- "I'll take the prisoner downstairs," said Tom condescendingly.
- "I love reading *Moby Dick*," said Tom superficially.
- "My glasses are fogged up," said Tom optimistically.
- "Are there any questions?" said Tom wisely.
- "I'll have the dark bread," said Tom wryly.
- "My stereo's broken," said Tom disconsolately.
- "My stereo's half fixed," said Tom monotonously.
- "My stereo's finally fixed," said Tom ecstatically.
- "My family has a great future," said Tom clandestinely.
- "The maid has the night off," said Tom helplessly.
- "Look at those newborn kittens," said Tom literally.
- "I love watching movie actresses," said Tom figuratively.
- "I'm reading about communism," said Tom readily.
- "I passed my electrocardiogram," said Tom wholeheartedly.

- "I used to be a conductor," said Tom extraneously.

- "Ships ahoy," said Tom fleetingly.

- "Care for some pudding?" said Tom hastily.

- "My blood pressure doesn't register," said Tom impulsively.

- "I need to go and convalesce," said Tom hospitably.

- "The doctors have discharged me," said Tom impatiently.

- "What I do best on camping trips is sleep," said Tom intently.

- "I'm a softball pitcher," said Tom underhandedly.

- "I've lost my flower," said Tom lackadaisically.

- "I'll have to take the telegrapher's test again," said Tom remorsefully.

- "I'm going to kill Dracula," said Tom painstakingly.

- "I've dropped my toothpaste," said Tom crestfallen.

- "I just swallowed a fishing lure," said Tom with bated breath.

- "Ben Hogan recovered his golf ball," said Tom profoundly.

- "Frankly, my dear, I don't give a damn," said Tom rhetorically.

Now that you see how the Tom Swifty game works, match each statement in the left-hand column with the profoundly swift adverb in the right-hand column. Answers to all games in this chapter are available in the back of this book.

Said Tom . . .

1. "I must attend my flock,"   apparently
2. "My pencil is dull,"   cryptically
3. "That makes 144,"   delightedly
4. "Plenty of starch, please,"   dryly
5. "She tore my valentine in two," fluently
6. "Let's visit the tombs,"   grossly
7. "I love hockey,"   halfheartedly
8. "I'm a ditch digger,"   ideally
9. "I have eight children,"   infectiously
10. "I'm a lion hunter,"   listlessly
11. "I flunked my exam,"   moodily
12. "I'll clean the chimney,"   pointlessly
13. "Pass me the cards,"   pridefully
14. "Whoops, another power failure," puckishly
15. "I've come down with measles," ravenously
16. "I've inherited a fortune,"   sheepishly
17. "Please mix me a martini,"   stiffly
18. "I love eating crow,"   testily
19. "I've lost my shopping notes," trenchantly
20. "I milk cows,"   willfully

A close cousin to the Tom Swifty is the Croaker, invented by Roy Bongartz. Croakers are like Tom Swifties, except that the verb, rather than the adverb, supplies the pun:

- "My pet frog died," Tom croaked.
- "I love cats," Tom mused.
- "I love beagles," Tom dogmatized.
- "That's no beagle; that's a mongrel," Tom muttered.

- "I used to be a miner," Tom exclaimed.
- "You're a wicked glutton," Tom insinuated.
- "I hate sweet potatoes," Tom yammered.
- "She must be wearing mink," Tom inferred.
- "I like Chinese detective movies," Tom chanted.
- "The little demon was deceitful," Tom implied.
- "I feel empty inside," Tom hollered.
- "I'll take the girl to the dance," Tom promised.
- "I'll glue the sheets of wood back together," Tom replied.
- "I've spotted more blackbirds than you have," Tom crowed.
- "The male sheep was badly cut," Tom rambled.
- "Look at my shiny kitchen floor," Tom waxed enthusiastically.

Now that you've seen some classic Croakers, match each statement in the left-hand column with the appropriate verb in the right-hand column.

Tom . . .

21. "We've taken over the government,"	bawled
22. "Company's coming,"	coaxed
23. "I've struck oil!"	cooed
24. "I'll corroborate that again,"	deduced
25. "I'm singing well these days,"	explained
26. "I travel all over America,"	guessed
27. "I used to be a pilot,"	gushed
28. "Take me to the dance,"	intoned
29. "My ad,"	reproved
30. "Have another soft drink,"	stated

Finally, and most pyrotechnically of all, is the Double Croaker, in which both the verb and the adverb or the verb and the noun unite to ignite the sentence:

- "Where did you get that meat?" Tom bridled hoarsely.
- "This meat is hard to chew," Tom beefed jerkily.
- "I train big cats," Tom lionized categorically.
- "I still think I can draw blood from you," Tom probed vainly.
- "Here's the story of the Liberty Bell," Tom told appealingly.
- "I have grape beverages," Tom whined with clarity.
- "I think I'll end it all," Sue sighed.
- "I've got a new game," mumbled Peg.
- "I hate reading Victor Hugo," said Les miserably.
- "I ordered chocolate, not vanilla," I screamed.

Can you croak doubly? Match each statement in the left-hand column with the appropriate words in the middle and right-hand columns.

Tom . . .

31. "Get me off this horse!" | added | blubberingly
32. "I plan to work in a cemetery," | barked | cruelly
33. "Go away, you snake!" | bellowed | doggedly
34. "My giant sea creature died," | derided | gravely
35. "You're a mangy cur," | expounded | greatly

RICHARD LEDERER   79

36. "The fire's going out!" needled   off

37. "I'm a mathemati-
    cian,"   plotted   softly

38. "I've lost a lot of
    weight,"   rattled   summarily

39. "Your embroidery is
    sloppy,"   spoke   thinly

40. "My bicycle wheel is
    melting,"   wailed   woefully

*Die, my dear doctor? That's the
last thing I shall do!*
> last words of Viscount
> Henry Palmerston

Never Say Die

When General Douglas MacArthur retired from military life in 1951, he declaimed the famous line: "Old soldiers never die – they just fade away." But Five-Star Army Generals aren't the only ones who never say die. As you read the variations that follow, remember that old punsters never die – they just come to the end of the punch line.

- Old milkmaids never die – they just kick the bucket.

- Old shoemakers never die – they just go to Boot Hill.

- Old plumbers never die – they just get out of sink and go down the drain.

- Old gravediggers never die – they just spade away.

- Old statisticians never die – they just get broken down by age, sex, and marital status.

- Old bus drivers never die – they just take a turn for the worse.

- Old mediums never die – they just give up the ghost and lose their spirits.

- Old reporters never die – they just meet their deadlines.

- Old postal workers never die – they just lose their ZIP and feel out of sorts.

- Old can collectors never die – they just go to the redemption center.
- Old librarians never die – they just become overdue and lose their circulation.
- Old proctologists never die – they just face the end.
- Old contortionists never die – they just meet their end.
- Old Egyptian tourists never die – they just go senile.
- Old Helsinki tourists never die – they just vanish into Finn Air.
- Old gardeners never die – they just go to seed.
- Old lawyers never die – they just lose their appeal.
- Old mimes never die – they're just never heard from again.
- Old chauffeurs never die – they just turn into garages.
- Old classicists never die – they just keep declining.
- Old fisherman never die – they just smell that way.
- Old taxidermists never die – they just begin a gnu.
- Old crossword puzzlers never die – they just go across and down.
- Old dairy farmers never die – they just go to the udder place.
- Old cartoonists never die – they just draw their last breath and go into a state of suspended animation.

- Old hairdressers never die—they just curl up and dry.

- Old mountaineers never die—they just come to the end of their rope.

- Old principals never die—they just lose their faculties.

- Old teachers never die—they just grade away and lose their class.

- Old housemaids never die—they just return to dust.

- Old Siamese twins never die—they just join the dear departed.

- Old Kurds never die—they just lose their way.

- Old hypochondriacs never die—they just imagine it.

- Old monarchs never die—they're just throne away.

- Old auto mechanics never die—they just become exhausted and get retired.

- Old church builders never die—they just expire.

- Old clock makers never die—they just get run down.

- Old calliope players never die—they just run out of steam.

- Old meteorologists never die—they just get under the weather with a 30 percent chance of clearing up.

- Old ranchers never die—they just breed their last.

- Old Wallaces never die—they just get listless.

- Old electricians never die—they just lose their spark.

- Old mathematicians never die—they just go off on a tangent.

- Old logicians never die—they just vacate the premises.

- Old firefighters never die—they just pull up their hose.

- Old sailors never die—they just get a little dinghy.

- Old psychiatrists never die—they just shrink away.

- Old interpreters never die—they just lose a lot in translation.

- Old gamblers never die—they just crap out and cash in their chips for another paradise.

- Old lumberjacks never die—they just split.

- Old game show hosts never die—they will be back after these messages.

- And, of course, old movie stars never die—they just fade away.

Had enough? No? Good. Fill in the blanks in each item of the diehard quiz that follows. Then check your results with the suggested answers in the back.

1. Old skiers never die—they just _____.

2. Old gangsters never die—they just go to the _____.

3. Old Australians never die—they just end up _____.

4. Old grammarians never die—they just lose their verb and slip into a _____.

5. Old population experts never die—they just take leave of their _____.

6. Old violinists never die—they just become _____.

7. Old quarterbacks never die—they just _____.

8. Old florists never die—they just rest on their _____.

9. Old sausage makers never die—they just take a turn for the _____.

10. Old accountants never die—they just lose their _____.

11. Old tree surgeons never die—they just take a final _____.

12. Old growers never die—they just turn into _____.

13. Old archaeologists never die—they just meet their _____.

14. Old organists never die—they just come to a _____.

15. Old cosmeticians never die—they just take a _____.

16. Old candle makers never die—they just get _____.

17. Old bathers never die—they just _____ away.

18. Old chemists never die—they just stop _____.

19. Old barbers never die—they just have close _____.

20. Old typists never die—they just lose their _____.

A pun is not bound by the laws which limit nicer wit. It is a pistol let off at the ear, not a feather to tickle the intellect.

Charles Lamb

Firing and Hiring

Nobody gets fired anymore. Nowadays, when people lose their jobs, they are "reclassified," "deselected," "outplaced," "nonpositively terminated," or any of a dozen other euphemistic verbs that really mean canned, sacked, or given the old heave-ho.

In the continuing search for newer, softer, more ambiguous verbs with which to administer the final blow to helpless jobholders, Laurence Urdang, editor of *Verbatim, the Language Quarterly*, announced in the Winter 1978 issue a new pun game.

"If clergymen are defrocked and lawyers are disbarred, how are members of the following trades and professions to be got rid of?":

- Alcoholics are delivered.
- Farmers are distilled.
- Hairdressers are distressed.
- Manicurists are defiled.
- Models are disposed.
- Mourners are decried.
- 9th-century Scots are depicted.

- Pornographers are deluded.
- Swearers are discussed.
- Wall flowers are decoyed.

Like "Never Say Die" and "Croakers," to which the *de-* and *dis-* game bears a family resemblance, Laurence Urdang's creation has provoked a passel of punnery. Here are thirty of the best worst:

- Ball players are debased.
- Bankers are distrusted and disinterested.
- Bigots are disintegrated.
- Caped crusaders are dismantled.
- China scholars are disoriented.
- CIA agents are despised.
- Cowboys are deranged, debunked, and decaffeinated.
- Dog catchers are debarked.
- Elks Clubbers are dismembered and dislodged.
- Feminists are deliberated.
- Feudal lords are demoted and distributed.
- Judges are dishonored, disappointed, and defined.
- Kings are desired.
- Magicians are dispelled and disillusioned.
- Mathematicians are deciphered, disfigured, discounted, and dissolved.
- Meteorologists are disgusted.
- Packers are desecrated.
- Pampered children are despoiled.
- Pig farmers are disgruntled.

- Plastic card users are discredited and discharged.
- Podiatrists are defeated.
- Potheads are disjointed.
- Preachers are demoralized, decreed, distracted, and dissected.
- Prospectors are disclaimed.
- Siamese twins are departed and despaired.
- Soldiers are defrayed.
- Songwriters are denoted and decomposed.
- Tailors are depressed, depleted, and dispatched.
- Teachers are declassified, detested, and degraded.
- Tennis players are deduced, disadvantaged, deserved, and defaulted.

Now that you see how *de*lightful and *dis*criminating the game is, try fashioning your own *de-* and *dis-* verbs to *de*scribe the *dis*missal of each of the following people. Then compare your creations with those in the back of the book.

1. Brides are _____.
2. Conductors are _____.
3. Fiancees are _____.
4. Fisherman are _____.
5. Poker players are _____.
6. Politicians are _____.
7. Sightseers are _____.
8. Stenographers are _____.
9. Telephone operators are _____.
10. Train engineers are _____.

Not done, no. For in a more optimistic vein we can use the prefix *re-* to describe what happens on that happy day when people are reinstated to their jobs or roles. Employing this formula, we can say that when upholsterers get their jobs back, they are recovered, shoeshine boys are rebuffed, sewer workers are recessed, poets are reversed, and exorcists are repossessed.

Here are thirty more rehirings:

- Baby food manufacturers are restrained.
- Baseball catchers are remitted.
- Cardiologists are repulsed.
- Carillonneurs are rebelled and repealed.
- Carpenters are replied.
- Cowboys are revealed and rebutted.
- Detectives are retrenched, retailed, and resolved.
- Exterminators are reproached.
- Eye doctors are recited.
- Fast food cooks are rehashed.
- Foresters are relieved and repeated.
- Founding fathers are reconstituted.
- Frankenstein is remonstrated.
- Geniuses are reminded.
- Grammarians are renowned and reverberated.
- Lawyers are retorted.
- Lion tamers are remained.
- Mashers are refreshed.
- Masons are relayed.
- Meteorologists are regaled.

- Morticians are rehearsed.
- Orphans are rewarded.
- Perjurers are relied.
- Postal workers are resorted and riposted.
- Poultry farmers are recouped.
- Prisoners are regarded and repented.
- Root beer salespersons are rehired.
- Seductresses are revamped.
- Shopkeepers are restored and retailed.
- Winos are reunited.

It's your turn again. Make up your own *re*-verbs to describe the rehiring of the following people. Once again, compare your creations with those in the back of the book.

11. Bikers are _____.
12. Choristers are _____.
13. Furriers are _____.
14. Knights are _____.
15. Lacrosse players are _____.
16. Rope makers are _____.
17. Shoemakers are _____.
18. Stevedores are _____.
19. Surveyors are _____.
20. *Ulysses* lovers are _____.

Not long ago, at a teachers' conference, I used the two games in this chapter to illustrate creative word play in the English classroom. Just as my speech ended, the lights suddenly went out and the assembled teachers were plunged into darkness.

Immediately a voice cried out, "We've been delighted!"

There followed a second voice: "No, we've been refused!"

And then a third: "How revolting!"

It was better than applause.

Iran. *A country between Iraq and Ihardplace.*

Johnny Hart
Wiley's Dictionary

A Daffynitions Fictionary

Some waggish genius once defined a bulldozer as somebody who sleeps through political speeches, and another verbathlete defined a buccaneer as the cost of a two-dollar pair of earrings. Punning definitions like these take a fresh approach to the sounds of old words. You won't find such entries in dictionaries, only in fictionaries, but they do have a name—daffynitions.

Johnny Hart, the creator of the comic strip *B.C.*, has long been a master of the daffynition. Part of the prehistorically contemporary humor of *B.C.* are the installments that feature *Wiley's Dictionary*:

- *abomination.* What a well-allocated nuclear arsenal should consist of.

- *asset.* A small donkey.

- *Demagogue.* The opposite of a Republigogue.

- *detour.* What you take to de museum.

- *hackneyed.* Why Joe Namath had to get out of football.

Tour de farces like these demonstrate the art of punupmanship at its highest—and lowest—and

Johnny Hart is only one of the many punsters to practice that art. Here are fifty of the greatest daffynitions ever punned:

- *acoustic*. What you play pool with.
- *acrostic*. An angry insect.
- *adamant*. The first insect.
- *alarms*. What an octopus is.
- *apologist*. A short summary of the first moon landing.
- *arrears*. What we should wash behind.
- *bambino*. Negative response from a mother deer.
- *bar stool*. What Davy Crockett stepped in.
- *beatnik*. Santa Claus on Christmas Day.
- *buttress*. A nanny goat.
- *cereal*. The style Salvador Dali painted in.
- *coffee*. Snow White's eighth dwarf; Sneezy's younger brother.
- *crick*. The sound a Japanese camera makes.
- *crocodile*. A jar of soap.
- *diploma*. Whom to call when a pipe leaks.
- *explain*. The simplest way to serve eggs.
- *forfeit*. What most animals stand on.
- *fungi*. The life of the party.
- *hijack*. A tool for changing airplane tires.
- *hootenanny*. Sounds made when an owl flies smack into a goat.
- *illegal*. A sick bird.
- *impeccable*. Never been kissed.
- *incongruous*. Where bills are passed.

- *insane*. Where French outdoor swimmers can be found.
- *jasmine*. An underground tunnel where people dig hot music.
- *khakis*. What you must have to start your automobile.
- *litmus*. Drunk rodent.
- *marigold*. Find a rich spouse.
- *metronome*. A city elf.
- *moon*. What cows are always doin'.
- *mutilate*. What cats do at night.
- *negligent*. Lingerie salesperson.
- *oboe*. An English tramp.
- *operetta*. Telephone company employee.
- *overbearing*. The cause of overpopulation.
- *pasteurize*. Too far to see.
- *program*. Metric advocate.
- *propaganda*. A socially correct goose.
- *romance*. Italian insects.
- *shampoo*. A fake bear.
- *shamrock*. A fake diamond.
- *specimen*. Astronauts.
- *stoic*. The bird that brings babies.
- *stucco*. What you get when you sit on gummo.
- *toboggan*. Why you go to an auction.
- *vice versa*. Underworld poetry.
- *vitamin*. What you do when guests come to your house.
- *wino*. What you do when you step on a small tack.

- *yellow*. What you do when you step on a large tack.
- *zinc*. Where you wash your face.

Interpreting and creating daffynitions exercises one's verbal muscles (mollusks) and sinews (misbehaving female sheep). Match each entry below with the appropriate daffynition that follows. All answers to the games in this chapter are in the back of the book.

announce   camelot   insecticide   mushroom
appeal   dandelion   kidney   novelty
assassinate   exchequer   laundress   ramshackle
behold   fodder   lawsuit   selfish
benign   hatchet   microwave   tulips

1. _____. What a hen will do with an egg.
2. _____. Frames for the mouth.
3. _____. Chain used on a billy goat.
4. _____. Swell king of the jungle.
5. _____. A small goodbye.
6. _____. One sixteenth of a pound.
7. _____. What we wish when we're eight.
8. _____. Judge's robes.
9. _____. An edible mollusk.
10. _____. Retired supermarket cashier.
11. _____. What the despondent ant committed.
12. _____. New beverage.
13. _____. Married to da mudder.
14. _____. What a banana comes in.
15. _____. Parking area for humped animals.

16. _____. Garb for a grassy area.

17. _____. Child's joint.

18. _____. Terrorist dined.

19. _____. What a bee wrestler uses.

20. _____. Where they make school lunches.

Now that you're all warmed up, try being a matchmaker for another twenty entries and daffynitions. These are somewhat harder.

aloof	biracial	dictum	innuendo
bacchanal	cello	dowager	lapse
banshee	condense	farcical	lever
bigamist	debate	humdinger	paradox
bigotry	denial	impunity	violin

21. _____. What we have when we sit down.

22. _____. Tuneful bell-ringer.

23. _____. Two physicians.

24. _____. Stag party rule.

25. _____. What you use to catch de fish.

26. _____. What a runaway husband does.

27. _____. Prom in a prison.

28. _____. How Jacob begat.

29. _____. Companions of Harry.

30. _____. Elf solidarity.

31. _____. Bad hotel.

32. _____. Long bike race.

33. _____. River Cleopatra lived next to.

34. _____. Stock market investment.

35. _____. German gelatin.

36. _____. Top of a Chinese house.

37. _____. Venetian alley.

38. _____. Instructions for Italian suppository.

39. _____. Fog over Italy.

40. _____. Italian redwood.

Now you are ready to make up your own daffynitions. Here are ten words for you to define punnishly. Compare your daffynitions for these words with those in the back of the book.

41. bacteria. _____.

42. cistern. _____.

43. city. _____.

44. furlong. _____.

45. goblet. _____.

46. locomotive. _____.

47. peekaboo. _____.

48. stagnation. _____.

49. sychophant. _____.

50. toupee. _____.

> *Science has not found a cure for the pun.*
>
> Robert Byrne

Figuring out Mathematical English

You probably think that mathematics and English have very little to do with each other. But, if you listen closely, you will find that mathematical concepts appear frequently in our everyday conversations.

Here's a chance for you to test your knowledge of mathematical terms, as well as your skill in fabricating outrageous and, for the most part, double sound puns. Use the list of mathematical words below to complete the statements that follow. Answers to the games in this chapter are in the back of the book.

Example: The *line* is the king of the jungle.

Mathematical Terms

acute	coincide	division	inverse
addition	concentric	elliptical	minus
apex	cosine	factor	multiply
axis	denominator	geometry	pi
center	dimension	hypotenuse	plus
circumference	divide	logarithm	polygon

polyhedron   rectangle   square root   tangent
postulate   rhombus   subtract   theorem
prism   secant   sum   trapezoid
protractor   slide rule   symbol   unit

1. A man lay out in the sun because he wanted to become a _____.

2. A missing parrot is a _____.

3. People often use _____ to cut down trees.

4. I don't want all the jelly beans, but I do want _____.

5. My favorite dessert is cherry _____.

6. Criminals usually end up in _____.

7. I'm not against using a tractor. In fact, I'm _____.

8. Square plants have _____s.

9. Her name was placed on the ballot by _____.

10. When the acorn grew up into an oak, it exclaimed, "_____!"

11. A child's face will light up at _____ of candy.

12. I bought my mother a book and _____ it by parcel post.

13. A banana is sure to make an _____ static.

14. You use yarn and needles when _____.

15. That's _____ little outfit you're wearing.

16. The zoid hunter hoped to _____.

17. If you need me to, I'll _____ your loan.

18. The poet wrote his love letters _____.

19. Eye glasses are good for _____.

20. The major leaguer got demoted to the
    _____.

21. While giving his report, the nervous student
    became non _____ sed.

22. For safety, every playground needs a swing
    rule, a see-saw rule, and a _____.

23. This _____ board consists of three layers.

24. Percussion instruments include the drum and
    the _____.

25. In Italy, I took a _____ to get to the
    Vatican.

26. "Please, Rick, say yes. Won't you _____?"

27. A musical group of lumberjacks plays in
    _____.

28. I love _____ open spaces.

29. Don't fill the glass above _____.

30. A bunch of cars all smashed together might be
    called a _____.

31. This priceless book is a first _____.

32. When the weather turns bad, I usually
    _____.

33. My explanation is perfectly clear. You can
    _____ you?

34. Cars are made in a _____y.

35. A book about submarines is a _____.

36. If the washroom upstairs is occupied, there is a
    _____.

37. A kiss might be called _____.

38. "_____," I complained to my tardy mail
    carrier.

39. When I tell my landlord to come and collect his money, I say, "_____."

40. "_____," said the woman, cautioning her parrot to listen carefully to President Reagan.

Now that you've explored the wonders of mathematical punning, here is a similar game that probes your knowledge of scientific terms, as well as your tolerance for unscientific puns. Again complete each statement by choosing a science term from the list below.

Example: A friendly country is an *alloy*.

Science Terms

atom	electron	oxide
Bunsen burner	element	periodic table
catalyst	fahrenheit	photosynthesis
cell	helium	phylum
centigrade	osmosis	valence
copper nitrate		

41. Eve's husband was called _____.

42. You place your magazines and journals on a _____.

43. The outer covering of an ox is the _____.

44. When Reagan ran for president, we were urged to _____.

45. What secretaries do with documents: _____.

46. What physicians do to their patients: _____.

47. An attractively tall person is _____.

48. A nickel a grade is more expensive than a _____.

49. A prisoner lives in a _____.

50. A dissertation about vice, with pictures, is a _____.

51. You keep track of cows and bulls on a _____.

52. You use a _____ _____ to set bunsens on fire.

53. Overtime pay for police officers is called _____ _____.

54. "_____," said the man who received the ten commandments.

55. An after-dinner candy eaten by an elephant is an _____.

56. A short drapery is a _____.

> *Punsters' minds work like Las Vegas one-armed bandits, with plums and cherries and oranges spinning madly upon someone's utterance, searching for the right combination to connect on a pun.*
>
> Robert Greenman

Anguish Languish

What do these four words mean to you?: *ladle rat rotten hut*. Most likely you find no more significance in the sequence than a random listing of four unrelated words. But try saying the four words aloud, stressing the first and third ones. Viola! Out comes something that sounds tantalizingly like "little red riding hood."

This kind of spectacular double-sound punnery is the topsy turvy stuff of *Anguish Languish* (English Language), by Howard L. Chace. In *Anguish Languish* (Prentice Hall, 1956), Professor Chace offers glitteringly new versions of furry tells (fairy tales), noisier rams (nursery rhymes), fey-mouse tells (famous tales), and thumb thongs (some songs) by replacing all the words in the original versions with words that are similar but never quite the same in sound.

Anguish Languish must be heard to be appreciated fully. Thus, you should read the following furry tell aloud to yourself or, better yet, to a receptive audience.

Here is Professor Chace's best known tour de farce, "Ladle Rat Rotten Hut," made famous when Arthur Godfrey recited it on television. A translation appears in the back of the book.

Oriole ratty? Den less gat stuttered! In English Language that means: Are we all ready? Then let's get started!

LADLE RAT ROTTEN HUT

Wants pawn term dare worsted ladle gull hoe lift wetter murder inner ladle cordage honor itch offer lodge dock florist. Disc ladle gull orphan worry ladle cluck wetter putty ladle rat hut, end fur disc raisin pimple caulder ladle rat rotten hut. Wan moaning rat rotten hut's murder colder inset: 'Ladle rat rotten hut, heresy ladle basking winsome burden barter an shirker cockles. Tick disc ladle basking tudor cordage offer groin murder hoe lifts honor udder site offer florist. Shaker lake, dun stopper laundry wrote, end yonder nor sorghum stenches dun stopper torque wet strainers.'

'Hoe-cake, murder,' resplendent ladle rat rotten hut, end tickle ladle basking an stirred oft. Honor wrote tudor cordage offer groin murder, ladle rat rotten hut mitten anomalous woof.

'Wail, wail, wail,' set disk wicket woof, 'evanescent ladle rat rotten hut! Wares or putty ladle gull goring wizard ladle basking?'

'Armor goring tumor groin murder's,' reprisal ladle gull. 'Grammars seeking bet. Armor ticking arson burden barter end shirker cockles.'

'O hoe! Heifer blessing woke,' setter wicket woof, butter taught tomb shelf, 'Oil tickle shirt court tudor cordage offer groin murder. Oil ketchup wetter letter, an den – O bore!'

Soda wicket woof tucker shirt court, end

whinny retched a cordage offer groin murder, picket
inner widow an dore debtor port oil worming worse
lion inner bet. Inner flesh disc abdominal woof
lipped honor betting adder rope. Zany pool dawn a
groin murder's nut cup an gnat gun, any curdle dope
inner bet.

Inner ladle wile ladle rat rotten hut a raft attar
cordage an ranker dough ball. 'Comb ink, sweat
hard,' setter wicket woof, disgracing is verse. Ladle
rat rotten hut entity bet rum end stud buyer groin
murder's bet. 'Oh grammar,' crater ladle gull, 'Wart
bag icer gut! A nervous sausage bag ice!' 'Better
lucky chew whiff, doling,' whiskered disc ratchet
woof, wetter wicket small. 'Oh grammar, water bag
noise! A nervous sore suture anomalous prognosis!'
'Buttered small your whiff,' inserter woof, ants
mouse worse wadding. 'Oh grammar, water bag
mousey gut! A nervous sore suture bag mouse!'

Daze worry on forger nut gull's lest warts. Oil
offer sodden throne offer carvers an sprinkling otter
bet, disc curl an bloat Thursday woof ceased pore
ladle rat rotten hut an garbled erupt.

Mural: Yonder nor sorghum stenches shud ladle
gulls stopper torque wet strainers.

Using "Ladle Rat Rotten Hut" for inspiration,
you may wish to make up your own Anguish Languish version of a furry tell, noisier ram, or thong.
Possibilities include "Dearth Ray Ladle Prigs,"
"Digress Upper Underpants," "Hunk Tie Dunk Tie"
and "Hurl, Hurl, Door Gong's Oil Hair."

*A good punster has to eider keep
puffin along or go loony when
people are robin him of his fun.*
John Rizzo

Pig Puns

Late in the summer of 1987 an unusual story appeared in the newspapers. According to international wire services, one Wang Xianfeng, the daughter of Chinese peasants, was neglected by her parents and brought up by pigs. While an infant, the girl was left to live with the family pigs, feeding on pig milk, crawling about like a pig, and in general imitating pigs. Happily, the same news story reported that Wang Xianfeng had been taken to a new environment and had been retrained to live a normal life.

But the story is not yet over.

Stedman's Medical Dictionary lists an ailment called witzelsucht (literally "wit seeking"), which is characterized by "a morbid tendency to pun while being inordinantly entertained thereby." As a terminal and interminable victim of witzelsucht, I am compelled to carry to its pig punnishing conclusion the saga of Wang Xianfeng.

If you have teeth, prepare to gnash them now.

Her Parents Were Swine

Once upon a time, a little girl named Wang Xianfeng was raised by pigs in a rural hamlet of China. Behaving porcinely, she grew up wearing cute little pigtails and porkpie hats, happy as a pig in spit when her relatives, sweating like pigs, carried her around the farm on piggy-back.

Devoted to the classics, they all spoke pig Latin.

Wang Xianfeng was an enthusiastic little pig gal. She squealed with delight over the works of Francis Bacon and went whole hog and hog wild for cartoon characters like Porky Pig and Miss Piggy, movies like *Porky's*, novels like *Swine Flu Over the Cuckoo's Nest*, and plays like *Pygmalion* and *Hamlet*, which she loved to ham up. Naturally she rooted for the Arkansas Razorbacks pigskin program and picked up their games on her ham radio set.

Xianfeng was an exceedingly moral person. She hated apartheid, especially when Boers discriminate against pygmies. She knew that the practice was a pigment of the imagination, a hogshead of hogwash that could ultimately hog-tie and stymie an entire country and leave it pork mocked and squealing like a stuck pig.

She never dated male chauvinist pigs who sell women a pig in a poke and then go squealing to their friends. One might just as well cast pearls before swine.

She also abboared swine who live high off the hog of pork barrel politics. Snout the right thing to do. It just isn't kosher.

Xianfeng did have her faults. She could be really pigheaded about her room, which could look quite sloppy, like a pigpen and pigsty. And at meals she could be a real boar, eating like a pig, hogging all the food, and having a swill time pigging out on the trough, the whole trough, and nothing but the trough.

I am hoping that my story of Xianfeng's life will

bring home the bacon for her. Then she can save her royalties in her piggy bank and eventually stuff them into her purse, which is, of course, made out of a sow's ear.

Is th-th-that all f-f-folks? Not in a pig's eye. The opportunities for more zany zoology are far too tempting. Supposing, for example, that Xianfeng had been raised not by pigs, but by various birds around the farm:

A Bird's Eye View of Wang Xianfeng

Once upon a time there lived a raven haired little chick who flocked together with her family like birds of a feather. Even though her life was for the birds, she had no egrets. She hung around with a bunch of turkeys and cuckoos, but she was always happy as a lark.

Every once in a while, Xianfeng laid an egg, but she never ate crow. She often parroted everything she heard, but she could talk turkey, too. She was kind of gullible, but she never swallowed cock-and-bull stories. Although at times she was a chicken who quailed, she could be quite cocky. And, despite going on many a wild-goose chase and running around like a chicken with its head cut off, she was really quite loosey-goosey and eagle-eyed.

Best of all, Xianfeng got to speak fowl language and pigeon English and never ever got ostrichized for it.

Or what if Xianfeng had been brought up by horses?:

Talking Horse Sense About Wang Xianfeng

Once a pony time there lived a coltish lass who grew up wearing a cute little ponytail and horsing around with her horsey family. Although she often said "neigh," she never bridled or kicked up her heels at authority. I've herd that she was a real workhorse who champed at the bit to get back in harness each day.

During her spare time she pricked up her ears at disc jockeys from Filly who played her favorite stable of stars, and she followed dark horse candidates who hoped to become frontrunners in the Gallop poll.

Xianfeng was nobody's foal. She knew enough to avoid stag fright, and she never beat a dead horse or looked a gift one in the mouth.

That's her story – straight from the horse's mouth.

And, of course, if Wang Xianfeng had been brought up by goats, she'd have been a cute little kid raised by a nanny . . .

> *I love puns so much that my wife made a sign I hang over my desk: CAUTION! INCORRIGIBLE PUNSTER. PLEASE DON'T INCORRIGE.*
>
> Bob Trowbridge

The Language Blender

My coming to St. Paul's School in 1962 happened to coincide with the arrival of a ninth grade student who turned out to be a pretty good artist. This young man became the cartoonist for our school newspaper, and for our yearbook he drew clever caricatures of every member of his class. After graduating from St. Paul's in 1966, he attended Yale, where his reputation as a tellingly witty cartoonist flourished.

The name of our famous alumnus is Garry Trudeau, and he is, of course, the creator of the comic strip *Doonesbury*. Not only were the seeds of *Doonesbury* planted at St. Paul's, but I believe that the name of the strip and one of its central characters also sprang from our soil. I posit this theory from two pieces of evidence. First, during Garry's stay with us, a social incompetent in St. Paul's slanguage was known as a *doon*. Second, Garry's roommate at school was one Charlie Pills*bury* (he of the doughboy family). My guess is that Garry threw the

two words into the language blender and from these ingredients whipped up the name *Doonesbury*.

Doonesbury preserves the spirit of Lewis Carroll, who possessed a particular aptitude for making up blends. Carroll called such inventions portmanteau words because he loved to cram two words into one as clothes are stuffed into a portmanteau, or traveling bag. Several blends from Carroll's "Jabberwocky" poem inhabit the lunatic fringe of the English language—*slithy* (*lithe* + *slimy*), *galumph* (*gallop* + *triumph*), and *chortle* (*chuckle* + *snort*).

Nowadays, when everyone tries to make everything as compact and efficient as possible, blends spring forth with a vigor that laughs at logic. Science generates *smog*, *escalator*, and *electrocution*, politics gives us *gerrymander*, *stagflation*, and *Reaganomics*, and *Time* magazine coins *ballyhooligan*, *cinemactress*, *sexperts*, and *sophomoron*.

Madison Avenue also churns out new blends, for a cleverly melded brand name proclaims in a single word two outstanding qualities that a product is supposed to possess. Thus, we imbibe Cranapple juice, Lymon drink and Nestea—and Schweppervescence may be lurking in our quinine water. We find Frogurt in our kitchens, Saniflush in our bathrooms, Bisquick in our cakes, Oldsmobility in our cars, Polishine on our shoes, Danskins on our bodies, and Dynamints on our breath.

It is easy to see that blends are like puns in that two words are pushed together so that the meaning of each is preserved within a smaller space than the two words would normally occupy. But, to qualify as true punnery, a blend must be funny as well as compact. Fortunately, enough humorous blends have been created to earn the genre a chapter in this book as a minor form of punnery.

Here are a dozen of the brightest examples:

- People who watch too many movies are cinemaddicts. Those hooked on television are videots.

- A lost weekend is an alcoholiday.

- Amateur athletes who sneakily receive money for their efforts have been called shamateurs.

- A McDonald's ad character is the Hamburglar.

- Movie marquees once advertised the sexploits of Barbarella.

- To expect a baby is to infanticipate.

- People who obtain quick divorces in Nevada are thus Renovated.

- Former live-ins sometimes receive palimony.

- A company calls its mistletoe Kissletoe.

- Complicated, nitpicking administrative procedures are labeled administrivia.

- What weighs two tons, feels cold, and comes on a stick? A hippopsicle.

- A busybody is a person with an interferiority complex.

> *"Language play is the new frontier of English."*
>
> Alleen Pace
> and Don L.F. Nilsen

Silver Spoonerisms

Perhaps you know somebody who occasionally says *revelant* for *relevant*, *aminal* for *animal*, *emeny* for *enemy*, and *pascetti* for *spaghetti*. Each of these mispronunciations illustrates a tendency to anticipate and, hence, to switch sounds within a word or between words.

When the effect of such a transposition becomes comic, we call the result a spoonerism, named after the Rev. William Archibald Spooner (1844–1930), once warden of New College, Oxford. Spooner is said to have set out to become a birdwatcher, but ended up a word-botcher. He became so renowned for his hilarious slips of tongue that he entered the immortal company of people like Charles C. Boycott, the Earl of Sandwich, and Amelia Jenks Bloomer, who have had their names eponymously enshrined in our vocabulary.

The first of Spooner's spoonerisms, and one of the few that have been authenticated, was spoken by the great man in 1879, when he was conducting a service and announced a hymn as "Kinkering Kongs Their Titles Take." Other switches attributed to Spooner, most of them spuriously, include:

- Three cheers for our queer old dean! (referring to Queen Victoria)

- Is it kisstomary to cuss the bride?
- The Lord is a shoving leopard.
- A blushing crow.
- A well-boiled icicle.
- You were fighting a liar in the quadrangle.
- Is the bean dizzy?
- Someone is occupewing my pie. Please sew me to another sheet.
- You have hissed all my mystery lectures. You have tasted a whole worm. Please leave Oxford on the next town drain.

There are two basic ways that spoonerisms are created. The most common method is to transpose parts of words:

- The suntan product Tanfastic.
- Psychologist: a person who pulls habits out of rats.
- What do you call a carpenter from Salt Lake City? A Morman Nailer.
- Trashy paperbacks come from the trite side of the racks.
- A good masseur leaves no stern untoned.
- A man who hated seabirds left no tern unstoned.
- A baker used a special, multi-bladed cutting instrument and called it a four loaf cleaver.
- Combined charity drives put all the begs in one ask-it.
- When a Japanese car factory blew up, it began raining Datsun cogs.

- When Dow Chemical was manufacturing napalm, the company was known as the Callous Dowboys.
- One blackbird to another: Bred any good rooks lately?
- Sign on a bar: Our customers enter optimistically and leave misty optically.
- I'd rather have a bottle in front of me than a frontal lobotomy.

A second popular method of spoonerizing is to transpose whole words:

- Time wounds all heels. — Groucho Marx
- Television: A set of tireless tubes.
- Hangover: The wrath of grapes.
- Snuff salesman: One who sticks his business in other people's noses.
- Budgie: Mother's whistler.
- Olympic officials: The souls that time men's tries.
- Alimony: The bounty of mutiny.
- It's not the men in your life that count — it's the life in your men. — Mae West
- One frog to another: Time's fun when you're having flies.
- Ecologists believe that a bird in the bush is worth two in the hand.
- Slogan for a feminist work stoppage: Don't iron while the strike is hot.
- The Oakland football stadium is the Ark of the Lost Raiders.
- A cannibal gave his wife for her birthday a box of Farmer's Fannies.

- Walter Winchell said that he never panned the opening show of a new theater season because he didn't want to stone the first cast.

- A bunch of cattle put into a satellite was called the herd shot round the world.

- Work is the ruin of the drinking classes. — Oscar Wilde

Spoonerisms qualify as punnery because they humorously compact two or more meanings in exactly half the space that they would normally occupy. One of the cleverest transpositions ever uttered transpired when an elderly man neglected to rise when a stout woman entered the room. She chided him: "I see you are not so gallant as when you were a boy." He retorted: "And I see you are not so buoyant as when you were a gal."

The most gut-busting example of extended sound switching is associated with Colonel Lemuel Q. Stoopnagle of the old radio team of Stoopnagel and Bud:

Prinderella and the Cince

Twonce upon a wime there lived a cincess named Prinderella. She lived with her sticked wepmother and her sugly isters. They made her pine all the shots and shans and do all the wirty dirk around the house.

Isn't that a shirty dame?

One day the ping issued a croclamation that all the geligible irls in the kingdom should come to a drancy fess ball. Prinderella didn't have a drancy fess. All she had was an irty drag.

Isn't that a shirty dame?

So off went the three sugly isters and the sticked wepmother to the drancy fess ball while

Prinderella stayed home. Who should appear but her gairy fodmother, who quickly turned a cumpkin into a poach, four hice into morses, and Prinderella's irty drag into a drancy fess. But she told Prinderella that she had to be home by the moke of stridnight.

Isn't that a shirty dame?

Prinderella pranced with the dince all night long, but at the moke of stridnight she ran down the stalace peps and slopped her dripper.

Isn't that a shirty dame?

The next day the ping issued another croclamation that all the geligible irls in the kingdom should sly on the tripper. The three sugly isters and the sticked wepmother slied on the tripper, but it fidn't dit. Prinderella slied on the tripper, and it fid dit. So they mot garried and hived lappily ever after.

Many English speaking children first learn how to spoonerize by hearing and posing a special kind of riddle that begins with the formula "What's the difference between . . . ?":

- What's the difference between a mouse and a pretty girl? One harms the cheese; the other charms the he's.

- What's the difference between a pursued deer and an undersized witch? One is a hunted stag; the other is a stunted hag.

- What's the difference between a church bell and a pick-pocket? One peals from the steeple; the other steals from the people.

- What's the difference between a light in a cave and a dance in a bar? One is a taper in a cavern; the other is a caper in a tavern.

- What's the difference between a tube and a crazy Dutchman? One is a hollow cylinder; the other is a silly Hollander.

- What's the difference between a photocopier and the flu? One makes facsimiles; the other makes sick families.

- What's the difference between an oak tree and a tight shoe? One makes acorns; the other makes corns ache.

- What's the difference between a skilled marksman and the man who tends his targets? One hits the mark; the other marks the hit.

- What's the difference between a dentist and a New York baseball fan? One yanks for the roots; the other roots for the Yanks.

Now it's time for you to splay a pame of goonerisms – oops, I mean play a game of spooner-isms. Using the definitions and clues provided below, fill in the blanks to complete each spooner-ized expression. I guarantee that this exercise will warm your mart and hind and tickle your bunny phone. Oh, oh, I mean your heart and mind and funny bone. Answers appear in the last section of this book.

Example: A rapidly moving feline is a *running cat*, while a clever rodent is a *cunning rat*.

1. An adorable glove is a cute _____.

   A silent baby cat is a _____ _____.

2. A sweet toothed grizzly is a honey _____.

   Rabbit fur is _____ _____.

3. Chilly lasses are cold _____.

   Blonde ringlets are _____ _____.

4. A fisherman baits his _____.
   A lazy schoolboy _____ his _____.
5. A large needle is a big _____.
   Hogs eat out of a _____ _____.
6. A rundown hotel is a flea _____.
   A wasp's banner is a _____ _____.
7. An auto cooler is a car _____.
   A distant container is a _____ _____.
8. A well-brushed equine is a curried _____.
   Rapid teaching makes for a _____ _____.
9. Two pairs of hosiery are four _____.
   A hurting vulpine is a _____ _____.
10. A destructive mule is a mangling _____.
    A hanging chimp is a _____ _____.
11. An ale container is a beer _____.
    A small insect is a _____ _____.
12. Dark cows are brown _____.
    A war for the throne is a _____ _____.
13. Rotten lettuce makes a bad _____.
    A depressing song is a _____ _____.
14. A jammed entrance is a stuck _____.
    A place that sells quackers is a _____ _____.
15. Romeo and Juliet shared a doomed _____.
    A woven pigeon is a _____ _____.

16. If you like books, you have a reading
    _____.
    A prudent bunny is a _____ _____.
17. Half a cleaning tool is a partial _____.
    A military father is a _____ _____.
18. A flaming seat is a burning _____.
    A stirring grizzly is a _____ _____.
19. A granny is a born _____.
    A granary is a _____ _____.
20. A rodent chronicle is a mouse _____.
    A puzzle you do at home is a _____
    _____.
21. An unwelcome party guest is a gate
    _____.
    One who smashes boxes is a _____
    _____.
22. You shop for a toothbrush in a dental
    _____.
    A brainy missile is a _____ _____.
23. Talking birds place their soda glasses on parrot
    _____.
    Large pictures of vegetables are _____
    _____.
24. A jumping sorcerer is a leaping _____.
    A crying reptile is a _____ _____.
25. A lashing monster serpent is a whipping
    _____.
    A leaky cart is a _____ _____.
26. A web-spinning bibliophile is a reading
    _____.
    A swift cyclist is a _____ _____.

27. Rabbit periodicals are bunny _____.

    Sacks of coins are _____ _____.

28. Reactionaries are right _____.

    A piece of bleached jewelry is a _____

    _____.

29. A facetious sea lion is a winking _____.

    A drowning car support is a _____

    _____.

30. Thomas's English Muffins have nooks and

    _____.

    Thieves and governesses are _____ and

    _____.

Punning is a talent which no man affects to despise, but he that is without it.

Jonathan Swift

A Round of Set-Ups

An ancient jungle king tyrannized his subjects and forced them to build him one elaborate throne after another—first of mud, then bamboo, then tin, then copper, then silver, and so on. When the king became tired of each throne, he would store it in the attic of his grass hut. One day the attic collapsed, and the thrones crashed down upon the chief's head and killed him.

The moral of the tale is: People who live in grass houses shouldn't stow thrones.

You have just been the victim of a set-up pun, a conspiracy of narrative and word play. In set-up punnery, the punster contrives an imaginary situation that leads up to a climax punningly and cunningly based on a well-known expression or title. In a good set-up pun, we groan at the absurdity of the situation while admiring the ingenuity with which the tale reaches its foreordained conclusion.

I hope that this book has convinced you that a bun is indeed the doughiest form of wheat. Now it's time to wash down all those buns with a round of set-ups. At the end of each story you are asked to provide the *punch* line by filling in the blanks. As a review of the categories in this book, identify the major form of punnery in each punch line—

homographic, homophonic, double sound, or spoonerism.

Answers appear in the section coming up.

1. Rudolph, a dedicated Russian communist and important rocket scientist, was about to launch a large satellite. His wife, a fellow scientist at the base, urged Rudolph to postpone the launch because, she asserted, a hard rain was about to fall. Their friendly disagreement soon escalated into a furious argument that Rudolph closed by shouting:

"Rudolph _____!"

2. A congregation decided to paint the walls of the church. They were doing an admirable job until they began to run out of paint, so they decided to thin the stuff in order to complete their task.

Shortly after the job was finished, the rains descended from the heavens, and the paint began to peel from the walls of the church. And a thunderous voice boomed from above:

"Repaint and _____!"

3. In days of old when knights were bold, people were a lot smaller than they are today, so much smaller, in fact, that many knights rode upon large dogs when they couldn't get horses.

One dark and stormy night, as the rain blew about, a squire entered a pet store in order to purchase a large dog for his master, the Black Knight. Unfortunately, all the shopkeeper could offer the squire was one undersized, mangy mutt. Commented the squire:

"I wouldn't send a _____."

4. In Baghdad, a worthy young man named Abdul found a beautiful urn. When he began to polish the urn, out came a magnificently bearded genie, who introduced himself as Benny. Benny granted

Abdul the obligatory three wishes and bid him goodbye.

Abdul knew that if he could shave Benny's
beard, the genie would have to return to the urn and
grant him three more wishes. Wielding a magic
razor, Abdul shaved off Benny's beard, and, sure
enough, Benny flew back into the enchanted vessel.

Moral: A Benny shaved _____.

5. Roy Rogers went bathing in a creek. Along
came a mountain lion and began nibbling on one of
Roy's new boots. Dale Evans entered the scene,
pulled out her trusty rifle, and shot the lion. She
turned to her husband and asked:

"Pardon me, Roy, is that the cat that _____?"

6. In an ancient kingdom, the castle was sur-
rounded by a treacherous swamp called the Yellow
Fingers. Whenever the king would ask his lords and
knights to cross the Yellow Fingers, they would
reply:

"Let your _____."

7. A man purchased a cute little pet that was so
rare it was called a Raree. The pet turned out to
have a huge appetite, ate up all the man's food, and
grew to weigh a thousand pounds.

Finally, the man decided that he had to get rid
of the Raree by dumping it off a cliff. He loaded the
creature into a wheelbarrow and began the trek up a
hill to the cliff's edge. But the way was so long and
the Raree so bulky that the man had to give up. He
discovered that:

_____.

8. Mrs. Wong, a Chinese woman, gave birth to
a blond-haired, blue-eyed Caucasian baby. When the

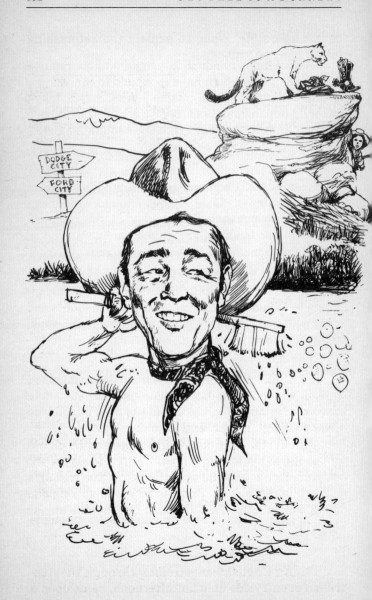

doctor asked Mr. Wong to explain the astonishing occurrence, he replied:

"Two Wongs _____."

9. A fisherman carelessly dropped his wallet into the water and was amazed to see a school of carp deftly balancing the wallet on their noses and tossing it from one fish to the other. "Gosh," exclaimed the fisherman, "That's the first time I've ever seen:

"Carp to carp _____."

10. To enforce the ban against exporting mynah birds, the State trained lions to guard its frontiers. One day two smugglers tried to sneak a mynah bird out of the country while the border lions were sleeping. But the lions woke up and captured the smugglers, who were accused of:

Transporting mynahs _____.

11. A father waited in line with his daughter Shelly for the chance to sign the White House guest-book. Impatiently the little girl pushed in front of a nun to get her turn. The father restrained his daughter and said:

"Wait till _____."

12. Three Indian women had babies. The first sat on a deer hide rug and gave birth to a five-pound boy. The second sat on a moose hide rug and gave birth to a six-pound boy. The third sat on a rug made of hippopotamus hide and had an eleven-pound boy. Which proves that:

The son of the squaw on the hippopotamus is equal to:

_____.

13. An Englishman, strolling through the Australian countryside on a hot afternoon, came upon a

Sisters of Mercy Convent. He asked to come in and requested a cup of tea. The abbess gladly agreed and explained that the convent was famous for its special blend of tea, which it made by boiling the juice of the Koala bear.

The Englishman took one sip of the tea and spat it out, spluttering that the hair of the Koala bear was floating around on the surface of his drink. "Of course," explained the abbess:

"The Koala tea _____."

14. A baseball umpire had a reputation for mean and surly behavior. One Sunday morning the umpire asked his son to jump on his lap and listen as the father read the son the funnies. But the boy refused because:

The son never sits _____.

15. A witch doctor kept the members of his tribe in virtual subjugation by means of his powerful magic. Whenever one of the tribespeople tried to revolt against the witch doctor, the tyrant would utter a magic incantation and turn that person into an apple.

One night a group of the doctor's desperate subjects sneaked into his hut, opened his book of magic recipes, and learned the apple incantation. When the doctor awoke, the people turned him into an apple.

But the magic book informed the people that, if the apple ever dried out and changed significantly in weight, the apple would change back into a doctor, who would take his revenge. So every day they would place the apple on a scale to make sure that its weight remained the same.

Moral: A weigh a day _____.

16. Sam the Clam ran a place that featured go-go dancing. After playing a gig at Sam's, the harpist

in one of the bands realized that he had forgotten to take his harp with him. Said the musician:

"I left my harp _____."

17. In Thailand there lived an old wood carver named Chan. He lived on the edge of a teakwood forest and earned his living by gathering wood and carving figurines to sell at market.

Deep in the same woods lived a large brown bear whose feet were shaped like those of a small boy. One day the bear broke into Chan's cabin and made off with several carvings that had been sitting on Chan's worktable.

Chan returned to his cottage just as the bear was running away, sized up the situation, and shouted:

"Come back! Boyfoot bear with _____!"

18. A group of chess playing fanatics would gather each day in the hotel lobby to brag about their greatest victories. Came a day when the hotel manager barred the group from the lobby because he couldn't stand to listen to a band of:

Chess nuts _____.

19. A Frenchman and a Czechoslovakian went out hunting for bear. When the two had not returned after four days, their friends, fearing the worst, went out searching for them.

The group came to a clearing, and, sure enough, they saw a mother and father bear each with a bloated belly. Slashing open the belly of the female, the distraught friends found therein the remains of the Frenchman. Their darkest fears confirmed, the group looked at the other bear and guessed:

"The Czech is _____."

20. There once lived a court jester who drove everybody crazy with his compulsive punning. One

day the king could stand it no longer. "Enough!" cried the king. "Hang the fool!"

But as the noose was being drawn around the punster's neck, the king had a change of heart; "I'll free you on one condition: that you never make another pun as long as you live."

"That I promise, your Majesty," said the jester: "No noose _____."

So they hanged him.

The Answers

The Time of the Signs (page 16)

1. pieces 2. road 3. antiquity 4. skid 5. star
6. prayer 7. faith 8. dye 9. Site 10. blades

11. time 12. tock 13. pool 14. lynx 15. false
16. wide 17. shaping 18. dents 19. bulbs 20. vine

Poetic Licenses (page 20)

The order of the answers is: 15, 1, 13, 12, 14, 3,
7, 4, 10, 11, 5, 8, 2, 9, 6

18, 17, 20, 16, 22, 19, 25 (excuse moi), 23, 24
(tennis anyone?), 21

Letter Perfect Words (page 22)

1. B (bee, be) 2. I (eye, I) 3. G (gee) 4. J (jay) 5. A
(a) 6. C (sea, see) 7. K (Kay) 8. P (pea) 9. O (owe, oh,
o) 10. T (tea, tee) = BIG JACKPOT

11. seize (C's) 12. tease (T's) 13. wise (Y's)
14. ease (E's) 15. use (U's)

16. empty (MT) 17. easy (EZ) 18. ivy (IV)
19. envy (NV) 20. icy (IC) 21. decay (DK) 22. kewpie
(QP) 23. cagey (KG) 24. excess (XS) 25. beady (BD)
26. seedy (CD) 27. Emmy (ME) 28. enemy (NME)
29. excellency (XLNC) 30. anemone (NMNE)
31. arcadian (RKDN) 32. expediency (XPDNC)

33. Casey (KC) 34. Elsie (LC) 35. Odie (OD)
36. Artie (RT) 37. Katie (KT) 38. Abie (AB) 39. Arby
(RB) 40. Emily (MLE)

Homographs: The Antics of Semantics (page 33)

1. ring 2. hand 3. set 4. blues 5. strike 6. top
7. ball 8. pants 9. rest 10. pitch 11. seal 12. fall
13. fire 14. pit 15. spring 16. court 17. plot 18. free
19. match 20. country

21. bluff 22. board 23. change 24. lash 25. pupil
26. pitcher 27. stake 28. dash 29. bill 30. coat

31. ace 32. tie 33. ruler 34. record 35. draw 36. jam
37. dart 38. litter 39. mint 40. file

41. soft 42. old 43. right 44. short 45. rough
46. odd 47. dull 48. free 49. take 50. poor 51. mad
52. lose 53. hard 54. present 55. fair 56. go 57. single
58. ill 59. minor 60. rare 61. fine 62. fast 63. fresh
64. partial 65. back

Homophones: What Do You Call a Naked Grizzly? (page 40)

1. does doze 2. hoarse horse 3. ant aunt 4. boar
bore 5. whale wail 6. hare hair 7. foul fowl 8. gorilla
guerrilla 9. dear deer 10. moose mousse

11. towed toad 12. cheap cheep 13. lynx links
14. lox locks 15. mussel muscle. 16. grisly grizzly
17. flees fleas 18. mule mewl 19. new gnu 20. ewes
use

21. paws pause 22. roe row 23. herd heard
24. tail tale 25. mite might 26. purchase perches
27. meet meat 28. pale pail 29. dual duel 30. genes
jeans

31. cellar seller 32. sweet suite 33. alter altar
34. isle aisle 35. plain plane 36. banned band
37. barred bard 38. sword soared 39. right rite
40. minor miner

41. base bass 42. tease tees 43. coax Cokes
44. thrown throne 45. whole hole 46. whirled world
47. sail sale 48. guest guessed 49. bolder boulder
50. flower flour

51. hoes hose 52. coward cowered 53. knave
nave 54. great grate 55. crew's cruise 56. idle idol
57. lessens lessons 58. manor's manners 59. vain
vein 60. principal principle

61. prophet's profit 62. steak stake 63. bizarre
bazaar 64. heals heels 65. pares pears 66. Sunday

sundae 67. one won 68. coarse course 69. morning mourning 70. pane pain

71. colonel's kernels 72. tacks tax 73. boy buoy 74. male mail 75. prince prints 76. choral coral 77. slays sleighs 78. maize maze 79. stationary stationery 80. naval navel

81. knight night 82. mustered mustard 83. sole soul 84. sees seas 85. eight ate 86. roomer rumor 87. bored board 88. boarder border 89. raise rays 90. sun's sons

91. Finnish finish 92. tied tide 93. lyre liar 94. patient's patience 95. cent scent 96. hear here 97. grosser grocer 98. better bettor 99. wine whine 100. booze boos

Don't Knock Knock-Knock Jokes
(page 46)

1. José 2. Henrietta 3. Wayne 4. Tarzan 5. Oswald 6. Della 7. Adelle 8. Raleigh 9. Isadore 10. Nicholas

11. Osborn 12. Amos 13. Andy 14. Ivan 15. Walter 16. Wendy 17. Dexter 18. Lionel 19. Sherwood 20. Barry

21. Freda 22. Phillip 23. Theresa 24. Ben Hur 25. Harry 26. Oliver 27. Eisenhower 28. Sarah 29. Arthur 30. Ira

31. Isabel 32. Desdemona 33. Humphrey 34. Sam and Janet 35. Keith 36. Yoda

37. hence 38. tuba 39. sofa 40. kleenex 41. ketchup 42. zombies 43. omelette 44. amoeba 45. lilac 46. toucan 47. radio 48. tequila 49. ooze 50. canoe

51. doughnut 52. eyewash 53. meretricious 54. cheetahs 55. fangs 56. aardvark 57. bay 58. despair 59. llama 60. event

61. effervescent 62. macho 63. catgut 64. hyena

65. cirrhosis 66. pecan 67. needle 68. censure
69. ammonia 70. baloney 71. manor 72. avenue

Punupmanship (page 53)

1. homophonic 2. homographic 3. double sound
4. homographic 5. double sound 6. double sound
7. homographic 8. homophonic 9. homographic
10. double sound

11. double sound 12. homophonic 13. homophonic 14. homographic 15. double sound 16. homographic 17. double sound 18. double sound
19. homographic 20. double sound

21. homophonic 22. double sound 23. double sound 24. homographic 25. double sound 26. homographic 27. homographic 28. homographic
29. homographic 30. homographic

31. double sound 32. double sound 33. double sound 34. homographic 35. homographic 36. homographic 37. double sound 38. double sound
39. homographic 40. homophonic

41. circuit 42. grab 43. anemones 44. hole
45. smoting 46. threw 47. amnesia 48. habit
49. hippo 50. mare

51. buoy 52. linoleum 53. pucker 54. hoe, hoe, hoe 55. rhyme 56. marmalade 57. towed 58. baited
59. saucers 60. leaving

61. cremated 62. Euripides 63. Eumenides
64. line 65. sheikh 66. Omar Khayyam 67. Juvenal
68. inhibited 69. heir 70. Abyssinia

71. marooned 72. Udder 73. meter 74. toot
75. Cairo 76. see 77. medication 78. pane 79. concrete 80. icicle

81. weenie 82. Dublin 83. sales 84. Mallard
85. peanuts 86. Abel; throne; tablets (two right gets you a point) 87. deck 88. pears 89. I owe, I owe
90. atmosphere

91. friar, monk 92. conclusion 93. steals
94. artery 95. Friday 96. melon-collie 97. read
98. some 99. temples 100. oboe

Have You Ever Seen a Horse Fly?
(page 66)

1. park 2. hop 3. flop, laugh, dance 4. rush, whip
5. call, fish, nap, nip 6. lift 7. sweep 8. clown, box
9. plant, roll, shampoo 10. hunt, trot

11. fence, party 12. snap 13. saw 14. cut 15. run,
park 16. punch, ring 17. sink 18. chop 19. deal
20. twist

21. fence 22. duck 23. bud, garden 24. bowl
25. box 26. shovel, storm 27. dance, deal 28. box,
clown, whistle

Jack and the Wonderful Beans (page 69)

Once upon a time there lived a boy named Jack
in the wonderful land of California. One day Jack, a
single-minded lad, decided to go forth to seek his
fortune.

After making sure that Jack ate a sandwich and
drank some Seven-Up and quinine, his mother ten-
derly said, "Toodeloo, toodeloo. Try to be back by
next Tuesday." Then she cheered, "Two-four-six-
eight. Who do we appreciate? Jack, Jack, yay!"

Jack set forth and soon met a man wearing a
three-piece suit and a toupee. Forthrightly Jack
asked the man, "I'm a Californian. Are you one
too?"

"Certainly," replied the man, offering the high
five. "Anyone for tennis?"

"Not today," answered Jack intently. "But can
you help me to locate my fortune?"

"Sure," said the man. "Let me sell you these
wonderful beans."

Jack's intuition told him that the man was a two-faced double-crosser. Tensely Jack shouted, "You must think I'm an asinine idiot who's behind the eight ball. But I'm a college graduate, and I know what rights our forefathers created in the Constitution. Now let's get down to basics about these beans. If you're intoxicated, I'll never forgive you!"

The man doubled over with laughter. "Now hold on a second," he responded. "There's no need to make such an unfortunate to-do about these beans. It's six of one and half a dozen of the other to me, but you won't find wonderful beans like this at the Seven Eleven."

Jack pulled out his trusty six-shooter and exclaimed, "I'll make you change out of that three piece suit and wear a tutu. Then I'll blow you to Timbuktu!" Jack then shot off the man's toupee. "Go away and recuperate at the Essex Hospital. But first I want you to give me the beans."

Well, there's no need to elaborate on the rest of the tale. Jack tenaciously zeroed in on the giant and won the battle for the golden eggs. He eliminated the big guy, and Jack and his mother were in seventh heaven and on cloud nine forever after – and so on, and so on, and so forth.

Tom Swifties (page 76)

1. sheepishly 2. pointlessly 3. grossly 4. stiffly 5. halfheartedly 6. cryptically 7. puckishly 8. trenchantly 9. apparently 10. pridefully

11. testily 12. fluently 13. ideally 14. delightedly 15. infectiously 16. willfully 17. dryly 18. ravenously 19. listlessly 20. moodily

Croakers (page 77)

21. cooed 22. guessed 23. gushed 24. reproved

25. intoned   26. stated   27. explained   28. bawled
29. deduced 30. coaxed

Double Croakers (page 78)

31. derided woefully 32. plotted gravely 33. rattled off 34. wailed blubberingly 35. barked doggedly 36. bellowed   greatly   37. added   summarily 38. expounded thinly 39. needled cruelly 40. spoke softly

Never Say Die (page 84)

1. go downhill 2. underworld 3. Down Under 4. comma 5. census 6. unstrung 7. pass away 8. laurels 9. wurst 10. balance
11. bough 12. vegetables 13. mummies 14. stop 15. powder 16. snuffed out 17. wade 18. reacting 19. shaves 20. touch

Firing (page 89)

1. dismissed 2. disconcerted 3. disengaged 4. debated 5. discarded 6. devoted 7. detoured 8. described, dispelled, denoted 9. disconnected 10. derailed

Hiring (page 91)

11. recycled   12. required   13. referred 14. requested 15. relaxed 16. recoiled 17. resold 18. reported 19. rebounded 20. rejoiced

A Daffynitions Fictionary (page 97)

1. hatchet 2. tulips 3. ramshackle 4. dandelion 5. microwave 6. announce 7. benign 8. lawsuit 9. selfish 10. exchequer
11. insecticide 12. novelty 13. fodder 14. appeal 15. camelot 16. laundress 17. kidney 18. assassinate 19. behold 20. mushroom

21. lapse 22. humdinger 23. paradox 24. banshee 25. debate 26. lever 27. condense 28. biracial 29. dictum 30. impunity

31. violin 32. farcical 33. denial 34. dowager 35. cello 36. aloof 37. bacchanal 38. innuendo 39. bigamist 40. bigotry

41. Where they serve germs 42. Opposite of brothern 43. One who is sat on 44. Angora cat hair 45. Young turkey 46. Crazy reason 47. Hide and seek for ghosts 48. Country of male horses 49. Ill elephant 50. Dutch treat

Figuring Out Mathematical English (page 102)

1. tangent 2. polygon 3. axis 4. sum 5. pi 6. prism 7. protractor 8. square root 9. denominator 10. geometry (gee, I'm a tree)

11. dimension 12. center 13. apex 14. unit 15. acute 16. trapezoid 17. cosine 18. inverse 19. division 20. minus

21. plus 22. slide rule 23. multiply 24. symbol 25. rhombus (Rome bus) 26. concentric 27. logarithm 28. divide 29. theorem (the rim) 30. rectangle 31. addition 32. coincide 33. secant 34. factor 35. subtract 36. hypotenuse (high pot in use) 37. elliptical (a lip tickle) 38. postulate (post, you late) 39. circumference (sir, come for rents) 40. polyhedron (polly, heed Ron)

Scientific English (page 104)

41. atom 42. periodic table 43. oxide 44. electron 45. phylum 46. helium 47. fahrenheit 48. centigrade 49. cell 50. photosynthesis

51. catalyst 52. Bunsen burner 53. copper nitrate 54. osmosis 55. element 56. valence

Anguish Languish (page 108)

Once upon a time there was a little girl who lived with her mother in a little cottage on the edge of a large dark forest. This little girl often wore a little cloak with her pretty little red hat, and for this reason people called her little red riding hood. One morning red riding hood's mother called her inside: 'Little red riding hood, here's a little basket with some bread and butter and sugar cookies. Take this little basket to the cottage of your grandmother who lives on the other side of the forest. Shake a leg, don't stop along the road, and under no circumstances don't stop to talk with strangers.'

'O.K., mother,' responded little red riding hood, and took the little basket and started off. On her route to the cottage of her grandmother, little red riding hood met an enormous wolf.

'Well, well, well,' said this wicked wolf, 'if it isn't little red riding hood! Where's our pretty little girl going with her little basket?'

'I'm going to my grandmother's,' replied the little girl. 'Grandmother's feeling bad. I'm taking her some bread and butter and sugar cookies.'

'Oh ho! Have a pleasant walk,' said the wicked wolf, but he thought to himself, 'I'll take a short cut to the cottage of her grandmother. I'll catch up with her later, and then – oh boy!'

So the wicked wolf took a short cut, and when he reached the cottage of her grandmother, peeked in her window and saw that the poor old woman was lying in her bed. In a flash this abominable wolf leaped on her bed and ate her up. Then he pulled on the grandmother's night cap and night gown, and he curled up in her bed.

In a little while little red riding hood arrived at

the cottage and rang the door bell. 'Come in, sweet-heart,' said the wicked wolf, disguising his voice. Little red riding hood entered the bedroom and stood by her grandmother's bed. 'Oh grandma,' cried the little girl, 'What big eyes you got! I never saw such big eyes!' 'Better to look at you with, darling,' whispered the wretched wolf, with a wicked smile. 'Oh grandmother, what a big nose! I never saw such an enormous proboscis!' 'Better to smell you with,' answered the wolf, and his mouth was watering. 'Oh grandma, what a big mouth you got! I never saw such a big mouth!'

Those were the unfortunate girl's last words. All of a sudden throwing off the covers and springing out of bed, this cruel and bloodthirsty wolf seized poor little red riding hood and gobbled her up.

Moral: Under no circumstances should little girls stop to talk with strangers.

Silver Spoonerisms (page 125)

1. cute mitten, mute kitten 2. honey bear, bunny hair 3. cold girls, gold curls 4. baits his hooks, hates his books 5. big pin, pig bin 6. flea bag, bee flag 7. car fan, far can 8. curried horse, hurried course 9. four socks, sore fox 10. mangling donkey, dangling monkey

11. beer mug, mere bug 12. brown cattle, crown battle 13. bad salad, sad ballad 14. stuck door, duck store 15. doomed love, loomed dove 16. reading habit, heeding rabbit 17. partial mop, martial pop 18. burning chair, churning bear 19. born kin, corn bin 20. mouse history, house mystery

21. gate crasher, crate gasher 22. dental mart, mental dart 23. parrot coasters, carrot posters 24. leaping wizard, weeping lizard 25. whipping dragon, dripping wagon 26. reading spider, speeding

rider 27. bunny mags, money bags 28. wing, white ring 29. winking seal, sinking wheel 30. nooks and crannies, crooks and nannies

A Round of Set-Ups (page 130)

1. Rudolph, the Red, knows rain, dear (homophonic) 2. Repaint and thin no more (double sound) 3. I wouldn't send a knight out on a dog like this (spoonerism, homophonic) 4. A Benny shaved is a Benny urned (double sound, homophonic) 5. Pardon me, Roy, is that the cat that chewed your new shoe? (double sound)

6. Let your pages do the walking through the Yellow Fingers (spoonerism) 7. It's a long way to tip a Raree (homophonic) 8. Two Wongs don't make a white (double sound) 9. Carp to carp walleting (spoonerism) 10. Transporting mynahs across state lions (double sound)

11. Wait till the nun signs, Shelly (spoonerism) 12. The son of the squaw on the hippopotamus is equal to the sons of the squaws on the other two hides (double sound) 13. The koala tea of Mercy is not strained (homophonic, homographic) 14. The son never sits on the brutish umpire (homophonic, double sound) 15. A weigh a day keeps the doctor an apple (spoonerism)

16. I left my harp in Sam Clam's disco (double sound) 17. Boyfoot bear with teaks of Chan (spoonerism, homophonic) 18. Chess nuts boasting by an open foyer (double sound) 19. The Czech is in the male (homophonic) 20. No noose is good noose (double sound)

THE INTREPID LINGUIST'S LIBRARY

PEOPLE SAY THE DARNDEST THINGS...

"Sir Francis Drake circumcised the world with a 100-foot clipper."

"In 1957, Eugene O'Neil won a Pullet Surprise."

"Illiterate? Write today for free help."

Don't miss these side-splitting treasuries from The Intrepid Linguist's Library...

☐ **Anguished English**
Richard Lederer 20352-X $5.95

☐ **It's Raining Cats and Dogs...and Other Beastly Expressions**
Christine Ammer 20507-7 $5.95

☐ **Get Thee to a Punnery**
Richard Lederer 20499-2 $5.95

At your local bookstore or use this handy page for ordering:

DELL READERS SERVICE, DEPT. DIL
P.O. Box 5057, Des Plaines, IL. 60017-5057

Please send me the above title(s). I am enclosing $_____.
(Please add $2.00 per order to cover shipping and handling.) Send
check or money order—no cash or C.O.D.s please.

Ms./Mrs./Mr. _____

Address _____

City/State _____ Zip _____

Prices and availability subject to change without notice. Please allow four to six
weeks for delivery.